KITCHEN SCIENCE

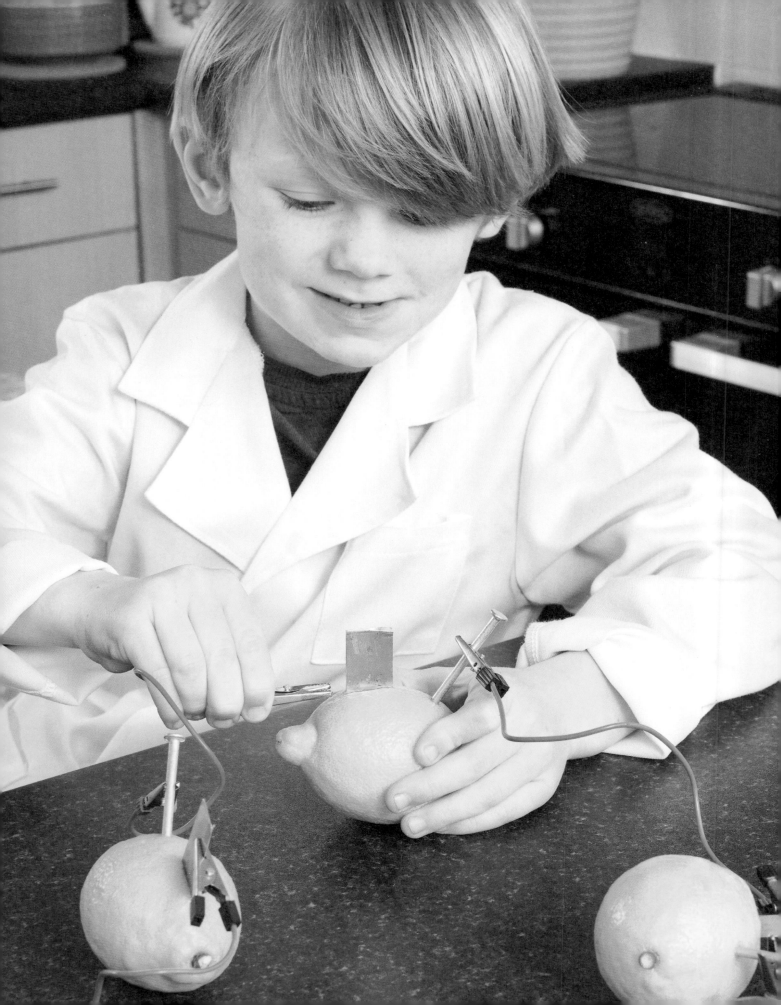

KITCHEN SCIENCE

30 AWESOME STEM EXPERIMENTS TO TRY AT HOME

Button
BOOKS

LAURA MINTER & TIA WILLIAMS

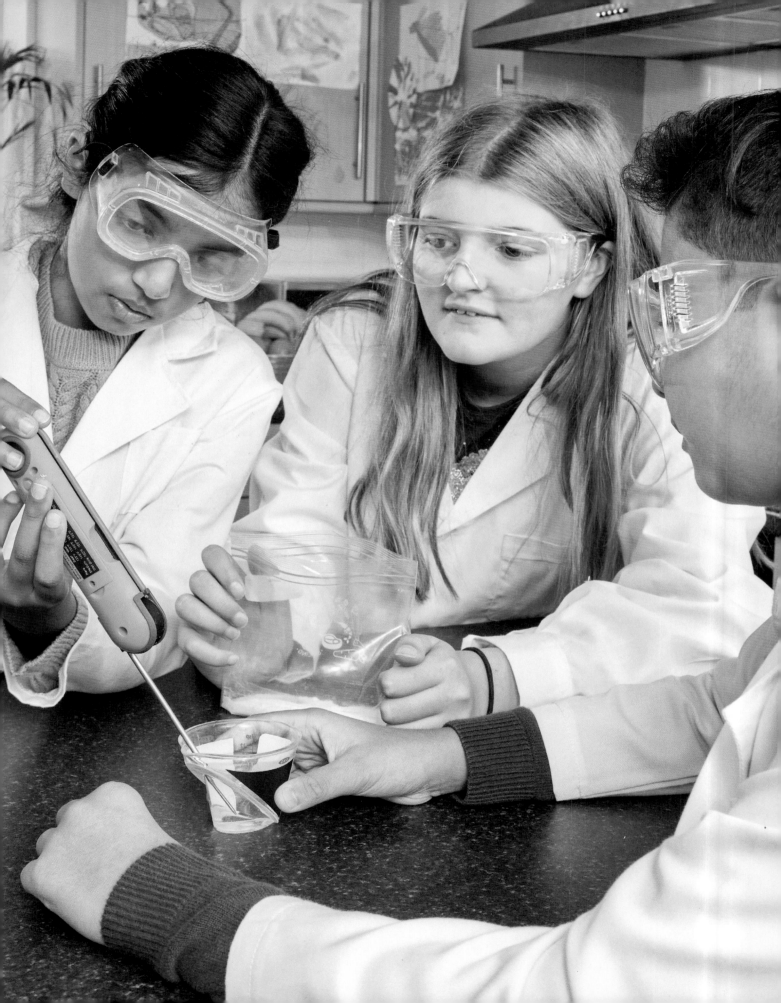

Contents

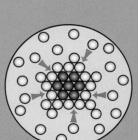

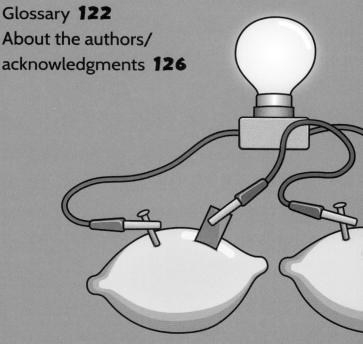

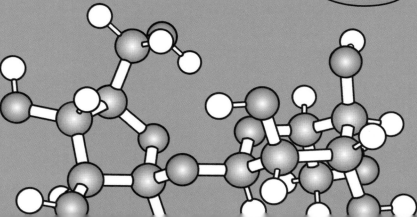

Introduction

The kitchen is the best room in the house, don't you think? Okay, maybe you don't agree with that statement yet but, by the end of this book, hopefully you'll be converted. We love the kitchen for all the yummy things you can make and the wonderful smells that make our tummies rumble. But what's amazing is that so much science goes on there, without you ever even realizing.

Have you ever thought about how magical it is to be able to take a whole bunch of simple ingredients and turn them into something delicious and totally different, like cake? Every time you bake or cook, there are many scientific processes and reactions going on that change your ingredients into something completely new.

This book will introduce you to some interesting (and a few very bizarre) science experiments that you can do using items you probably already have in your kitchen cupboards. Items that probably seemed very boring until now, like baking soda (bicarbonate of soda), cornstarch (cornflour), vinegar, or oil. Even with just those four ingredients there are tons of science experiments you can do.

Who would have thought you can generate electricity with a lemon, make ice cream just by shaking, or create powdered candy that fizzles on your tongue—all from the comfort of your kitchen? You will learn about how electricity is generated in the lemon battery project on (page 80), how osmosis can super-size your candy (page 40), what happens when you combine an acid and a base to make a lemon volcano (page 28), how wavelengths can make tasty cakes (page 52), and tons more. Plus, at the end you'll have a tasty treat or a cool magic trick to impress your friends with.

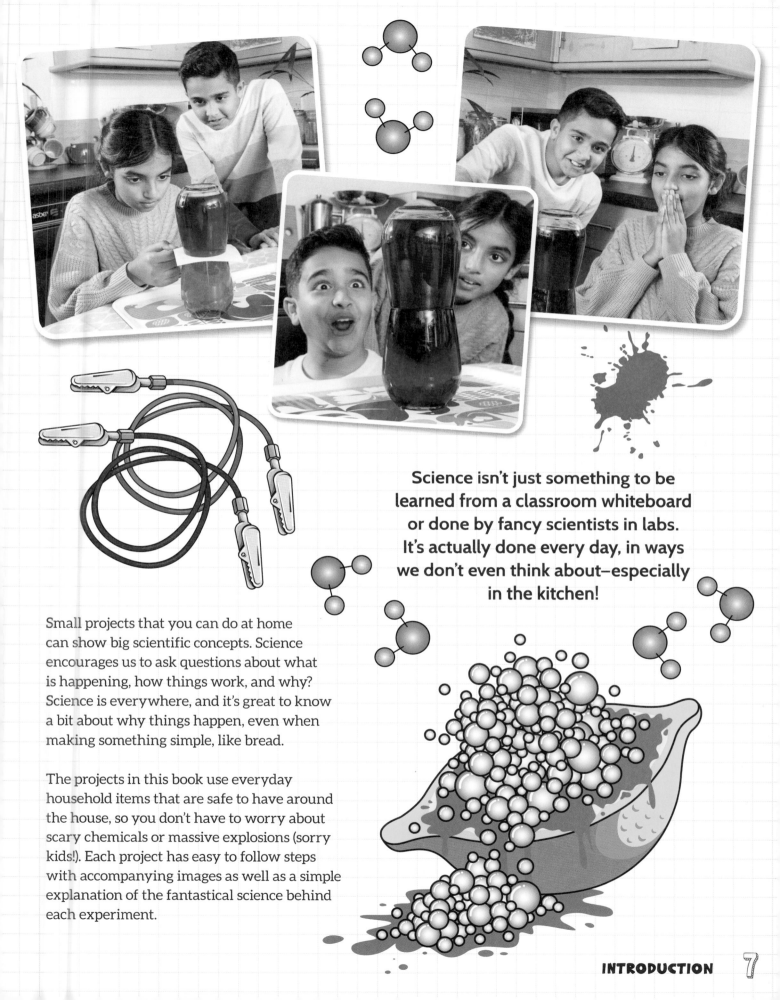

Science isn't just something to be learned from a classroom whiteboard or done by fancy scientists in labs. It's actually done every day, in ways we don't even think about—especially in the kitchen!

Small projects that you can do at home can show big scientific concepts. Science encourages us to ask questions about what is happening, how things work, and why? Science is everywhere, and it's great to know a bit about why things happen, even when making something simple, like bread.

The projects in this book use everyday household items that are safe to have around the house, so you don't have to worry about scary chemicals or massive explosions (sorry kids!). Each project has easy to follow steps with accompanying images as well as a simple explanation of the fantastical science behind each experiment.

Getting Started

Now you know that science doesn't have to done exclusively in a laboratory with expensive equipment. You'll already have most of the items for the projects in this book in your kitchen. Before getting started, flick through the book to familiarize yourself with what you will need for any projects you want to try out first. Below is an idea of some useful things to have in stock.

KITCHEN EQUIPMENT

It is useful to have clean, empty glass jars or drinking glasses, ice-cube trays, plastic jug, sieve, plastic funnel, saucepans, skillets, baking sheets, cookie cutters, and zip-seal plastic food bags.

FOOD ITEMS

Baking soda (bicarbonate of soda), food coloring, citric acid, vinegar, cornstarch (cornflour), and jello (jelly) powder are good science experiment staples. These items are great to have in stock for your science projects.

HOUSEHOLD RECYCLING

Your household recycling is a great resource for science. You don't need test tubes and beakers when you have plastic bottles and empty food jars. Throughout the book we've used glass bottles, plastic drinking bottles, soda cans, and lollipop sticks. These can all be rescued from your recycling bin to be repurposed into super science essentials!

OTHER ITEMS

Paint, paintbrushes, colored card stock, wooden skewers, and balloons will all be useful. For a very small number of projects, you might need to get some slightly more interesting items that are easy to buy if you don't already have them. For example, the lemon battery on page 80 uses some copper, galvanized nails, alligator clips with wires, and a small LED light. You can get these materials easily (and sometimes as a pack) online or from a hardware store. A thermometer is useful, but not essential, for the thermodynamic ice pack on page 114.

SAFE SCIENCE

Please note that adult help is needed for some of the experiments in this book. Some require use of an oven and hob, which must be done by an adult. We recommend wearing safety goggles. Some of the projects also need sharp knives for cutting up food items.

Ice Cream in a Bag

It takes just a few minutes to make this simple honey ice cream by shaking it around in a bag! Find out how it is done with the easy chemistry lesson, for some extra fun. For a lighter version, replace the cream with whole milk.

YOU WILL NEED

- ☑ 3½ fl oz (100ml) heavy (double) cream
- ☑ 3½ fl oz (100ml) whole (full fat) milk
- ☑ 1 tbsp honey
- ☑ About 2lb (1kg) ice cubes
- ☑ ½ cup rock salt
- ☑ Sprinkles, mini marshmallows, choc chips, or fudge pieces
- ☑ Jug
- ☑ Spoon
- ☑ 1 large and 1 small zip-seal plastic bag
- ☑ Warm gloves
- ☑ Towel
- ☑ Tub to store your ice cream in

1 Measure out the cream, milk, and honey and mix them together in a jug.

2 Pour the mixture into the small zip-seal bag and add 1 tbsp of fudge pieces, mini marshmallows, or sprinkles to the bag. Seal the bag well, squashing out any excess air.

3 Pour the ice cubes into the large zip-seal bag, it should be about half full. Add the salt, seal the bag, and then shake it vigorously to spread it all around the ice.

4 Put the small bag containing the cream mixture inside the ice bag and push it right down so that there is ice all around it. Seal the large bag, squashing out any excess air.

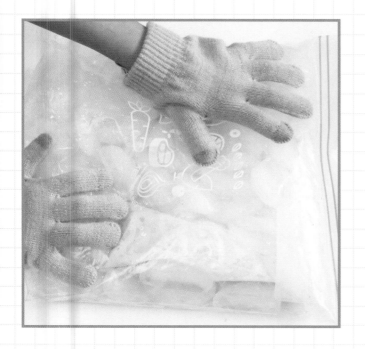

5 Put some gloves on as this bit gets chilly! Use a towel to mop up any condensation from the ice. Shake and squash the bags so that the ice moves all around the cream. Do this for five minutes. Shake shake!

6 After five minutes, remove the bag of cream from the ice. If the bag still feels floppy, pop it back in and shake a bit more until it feels more solid. Open the bag and turn out the ice cream into a tub. It may look a bit curdled to start with because ice crystals have formed but this will stir out and leave you with a lovely soft ice cream.

SCIENCE MADE SIMPLE

Isn't it cool how quickly you can turn a **LIQUID** into a **SOLID** just by shaking it? The salt is the key ingredient for this experiment. Without it, all you would have is a bag of cold, creamy milk. So how does the salt help? The salt causes the ice to start melting more quickly than it otherwise would, because the salt lowers the **FREEZING POINT** of water a little. As it melts, the ice takes heat from its surroundings—in this case, the milk. The ice pulls the heat from the milk and causes it to freeze. Mini ice crystals are formed in the mixture. Moving the bag around helps the milk mixture to freeze more evenly, while also adding air pockets to make it nice and light.

Have you ever seen trucks putting salt on the sidewalks and roads when it's icy? The salt helps to melt the ice quicker.

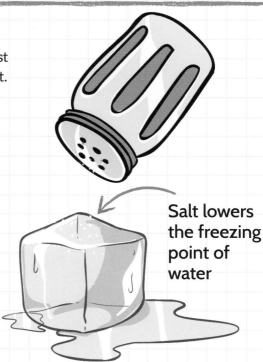

Salt lowers the freezing point of water

Super Strong Rice

Did you know that you can lift a bottle full of rice off the table using just a pencil? It's all thanks to the wonderful world of physics and friction. The coloring in this craft is optional but makes the bottle look decorative at the end.

YOU WILL NEED

- ☑ 3 cups uncooked rice
- ☑ 1 tsp white vinegar
- ☑ Bowl
- ☑ Spoon
- ☑ Zip-seal plastic bag
- ☑ Food coloring in various shades
- ☑ Kitchen towel
- ☑ Funnel
- ☑ Glass bottle
- ☑ Pencil

Tip

Use gel food coloring instead of the liquid type to achieve really vibrant colors.

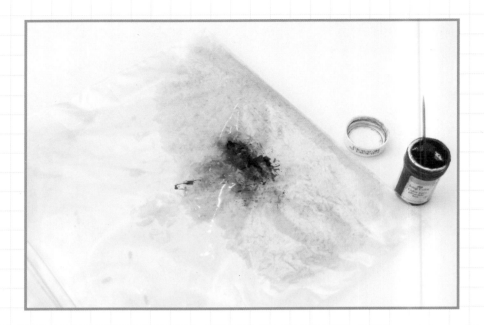

1 Begin by measuring out a cup of uncooked rice and add 1 tsp white vinegar. Stir to combine.

2 Put the rice into a zip-seal bag and add a little food coloring. Seal the bag and squish the rice around to mix the color through. Repeat steps 1 and 2 to make two more colors.

3 Tip each colored batch of rice onto kitchen towels, spread them out, and leave them to dry. They should be dry after a couple of hours.

4 Use a funnel to pour the rice into the glass bottle. You can layer the colors up or mix them all together.

5 Now for the science magic. Push the pencil into the rice, then pull it. What happens? The pencil will probably just come out of the rice again. Push it in and out a few times so that the rice starts to compact together. You should now be able to lift up the bottle of rice using just the pencil.

SCIENCE MADE SIMPLE

This experiment works because of **FRICTION**. This is a **FORCE** that reduces movement between two **SOLID** objects, like the grips on your shoes that stop you slipping over. Rough or bumpy surfaces have greater friction than smooth, shiny ones. The rough edges give something to grip on to.

When you first pour the rice into the bottle, there are gaps of air between the grains. But when you push down on the rice with the pencil, the air gets squashed out and the grains move nearer to each other. This makes them tightly packed in together, which increases the friction against the pencil. The rice pushes against the pencil and holds it firmly in place, allowing you to pick up the whole bottle with just the pencil.

Friction is created when the shoe moves against the bumpy surface

A smooth surface would not create as much friction

Sugar Crystal Swizzlers

These beautiful gem-like lollies are made from crystalized sugar. Learn how the sugar molecules behave to form these amazing shapes and then enjoy the swizzlers by sweetening desserts, drinks, or simply use as a lollipop.

Sugar molecule

YOU WILL NEED

- ☑ 1 cup boiling water
- ☑ 3 cups regular (granulated) sugar
- ☑ Jug
- ☑ 4 wooden skewers
- ☑ 4 clean champagne flutes, or small glasses/jars
- ☑ 4 different shades of food coloring
- ☑ Cocktail stick
- ☑ 4 pegs
- ☑ Greaseproof paper

Tip

Follow the steps carefully for best results. Bear in mind that the measurements need to be very accurate for this to work properly.

1 Add the boiling water to a pan over a medium heat. Add a cup of sugar to the pan and stir until dissolved. Continue to add the sugar to the water and stir until all the sugar has dissolved. This creates a solution fully saturated with sugar.

2 Turn off the heat and leave the mixture to cool for 20 minutes. While the solution is cooling, put a little sugar onto a plate. Dip the skewers in water, then roll in the sugar and leave to harden.

3 Rinse the glasses in hot water. Pour the solution into a jug then distribute evenly into the four glasses. Add food coloring to each one with a cocktail stick and stir well.

4 Add a peg to the end of the skewers and place them carefully in each solution. Make sure the sticks don't touch the glass.

5 Pop the glasses on a shelf and wait for the magic to happen! After a few hours you should start to see crystals forming. After about a week, the crystals should be growing on the skewers.

6 Once the crystals have grown, remove the skewers by cracking the sugar shell, which will have formed on the top of the solution with a skewer. Gently remove them and place on a piece of greaseproof paper.

7 Pour away the leftover syrup (see tip below). Rinse out the glasses, then place the crystal swizzlers back into the glasses to drip dry for a few hours. To remove any remaining crystals from the glasses, place them in a bowl of hot water and leave to dissolve. The crystals will keep well in an air-tight container for several months.

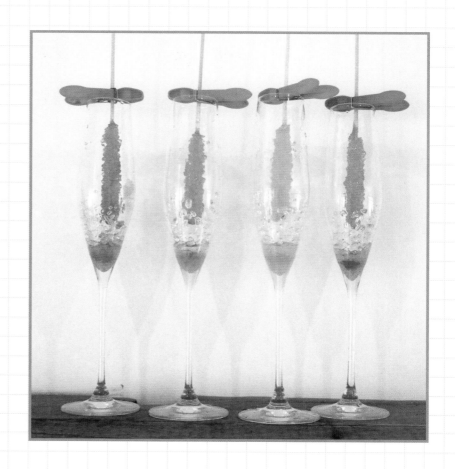

Tip

The leftover syrup is delicious as a sweet, sticky rainbow-colored topping for ice cream or waffles.

SCIENCE MADE SIMPLE

When you pour the sugar into the boiling water, you create a **SOLUTION** that is totally **SATURATED** with sugar. This means the water is holding as much sugar as it can. (You can also see this in action in the liquid density columns on page 110.)

The sugar **CRYSTALS** on the skewer are "seed" crystals. They start off the crystal growth by attracting other sugar crystals from the **LIQUID**. As the solution cools, the sugar **MOLECULES** start to collide and connect with each other. The crystals **DISSOLVED** in the liquid latch onto the seed crystals. As more and more attach themselves, the crystals start to grow and form this beautiful shape.

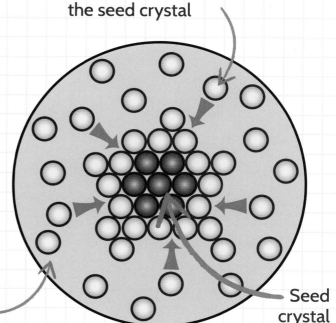

The sugar molecules connect to each other and stick onto the seed crystal

Saturated sugar solution with molecules moving around and colliding

Seed crystal

Honeycomb Candy Lava

*It's so much fun watching a liquid bubble up like lava!
Find out all about the chemical reaction that creates the bubbles
and then tuck into the delicious candy when you are finished.*

Safety note

This project involves bubbling hot caramel, which can burn you. An adult should help with that part of the recipe. Make sure you use a large pan for the caramel so that when it foams up it doesn't go over the sides.

YOU WILL NEED

- ☑ 3½oz (100g) superfine (caster) sugar
- ☑ 4 tbsp honey (or golden syrup)
- ☑ 1½ tsp baking soda (bicarbonate of soda)
- ☑ Large saucepan
- ☑ 3½oz (100g) milk chocolate
- ☑ Greaseproof paper
- ☑ Whisk
- ☑ Spatula

Tip

Use a mixture of half white chocolate and half milk chocolate for a marbled finish at the dipping stage.

1 Measure out the baking soda and get a whisk and spatula ready in preparation. Add the sugar and golden syrup to a large pan and cook on a low heat until all the sugar is completely dissolved. You can feel when the sugar grains have disappeared by scraping a spatula in the pan.

2 Once dissolved, heat the mixture for 2–3 more minutes until it darkens a little.

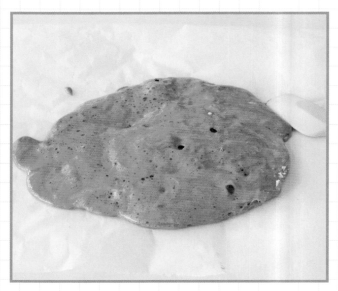

3 You need to move quickly for this part. Ask an adult to take the pan off the heat and pour in the baking soda. Whisk it in and watch as it rises up and turns into a bubbly, foamy monster!

4 While it is still bubbling, quickly scrape the mixture out of the pan and onto a piece of greaseproof paper.

KITCHEN SCIENCE

5 Leave the mixture to cool and harden, it should take about 20 minutes. Then break it into bite-size chunks. It should be full of lovely bubbles.

6 Break the chocolate into small pieces and heat in a microwave in 30-second blasts, stirring between each one, until melted. Then dip the honeycomb into the chocolate and place on greaseproof paper to set.

SCIENCE MADE SIMPLE

What causes all the little holes to appear in the honeycomb candy? When the baking soda is added to the hot caramel, the heat causes the soda to break down and release **CARBON DIOXIDE (CO_2)** as a gas. This is what makes it foam up and **BUBBLE**. The mixture then cools down quickly when it is poured out, causing the bubbles to be trapped as little balls of air in the caramel.

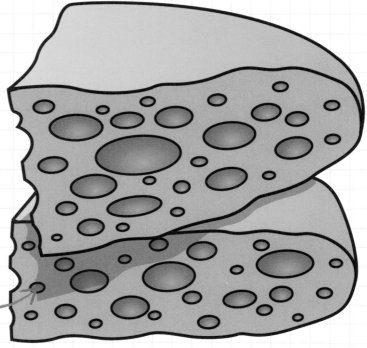

The tiny air bubbles are caused by CO_2 that is released when the baking soda is added

Dancing Raisins

This easy science experiment causes raisins to dance just by placing them in a glass of fizzy soda. Read on and find out why they sink when they first go in and what type of gas makes them rise up.

YOU WILL NEED

- ☑ Large drinking glass or empty jar
- ☑ Small handful of raisins
- ☑ Clear carbonated soda drink or soda water (e.g. clear lemonade)

Alternative

No soda in the house? No problem. You can make raisins dance using water, white vinegar, and baking soda (bicarbonate of soda). Fill a glass three-quarters of the way with water and stir in 2 tbsp of baking soda. Add the raisins, then slowly pour vinegar into the glass nearly to the top.

1 Fill a glass most of the way up with the clear soda drink.

2 Drop the raisins into the soda and watch what happens. The raisins will sink to start with but then you should start to notice tiny bubbles rising in the liquid and sticking to the raisins.

3 The raisins will start to rise to the top as if they are dancing and then fall back to the bottom of the glass.

Tip

Dried corn kernels also work well with this experiment.

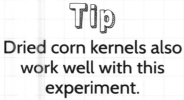

SCIENCE MADE SIMPLE

This experiment is all about **DENSITY**. This affects whether something sinks or floats in a **LIQUID**. The first thing that happens when you drop raisins into the liquid is that they sink to the bottom of the glass. This is because the raisins are more dense than the soda.

Soda is a carbonated liquid and has lots of bubbles, made up of **CARBON DIOXIDE (CO_2)**. The bubbles rise to the surface of the drink because the bubbles are less dense than the soda. They attach themselves to the raisins (the wrinkly surface of the raisins makes this easier) and make them float to the top of the glass. Once the bubbles reach the surface, the carbon dioxide is released into the air, the raisins can't float any longer, and sink back to the bottom of the glass. The pattern then repeats again as more bubbles attach themselves to the raisins and up they float again.

With the alternative mixture, a **CHEMICAL REACTION** happens between the baking soda and vinegar to create carbon dioxide bubbles, just like in the carbonated drink.

CO_2 bubbles attach to the raisins and lift them up

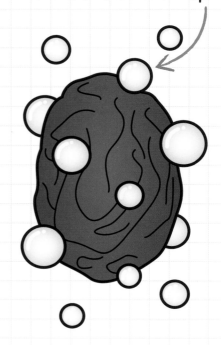

Lemon Volcanoes

This experiment looks and smells so good. We used lemons to make our mini volcanoes, but you can experiment with other citrus fruits such as limes, oranges, or even grapefruit to find out which one produces the most dramatic eruption.

YOU WILL NEED

- ☑ 2 lemons (or other types of citrus fruit)
- ☑ A few drops of food coloring
- ☑ Baking soda (bicarbonate of soda)
- ☑ Knife
- ☑ Lollipop stick
- ☑ Chopping board or plate
- ☑ Dishwashing liquid (optional)

Tip

To get even more bubbles, you can add a few drops of dishwashing liquid onto the lemon before adding the baking soda or squirt a bit of lemon juice on top of the lemon, once the reaction has started.

1 Start by rolling the lemon between your hands to release the juices a bit.

2 Cut the fruit in half widthways, then cut a bit off the bottom so that it stands flat.

3 Use a lollipop stick to squash the top of the fruit to release the juice.

4 Add a few drops of food coloring onto the cut part of the fruit.

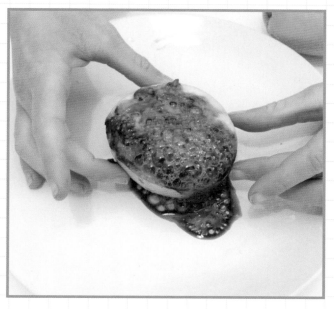

5 Add a generous amount of baking soda on top of the cut lemon and use the lollipop stick to work it into the flesh. This will get the reaction going! You should start to see a slow eruption of bubbling color.

6 To keep the reaction going give the fruit a squeeze.

SCIENCE MADE SIMPLE

The juice of a lemon is made up of an **ACID**, called citric acid (which is why these bitter fruits are called citrus fruits). Baking soda is a **BASE**. When the acid and base mix together, a chemical reaction occurs. This reaction causes a gas called **CARBON DIOXIDE (CO_2)** to be released, which makes the lemon fizz and bubble.

The citric acid in the lemon mixes with the baking soda

A chemical reaction creates fizzy bubbles of CO_2

Milk Plastic Fridge Magnets

Can you believe you can make a plastic-like substance from milk? This is how plastic used to be made before other techniques were invented in the 1940s. The best part is that this bioplastic will last for ages and ages and is biodegradable.

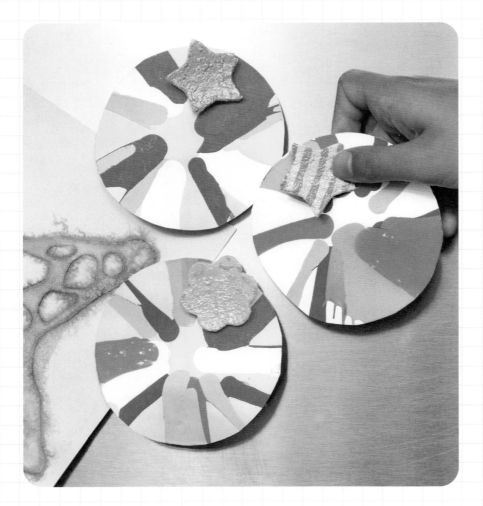

YOU WILL NEED

- ☑ 2 cups (450ml) skimmed (fat-free) milk
- ☑ 1½ fl oz (40ml) white vinegar
- ☑ Saucepan
- ☑ Greaseproof paper
- ☑ Rolling pin
- ☑ Small cookie cutters
- ☑ Kitchen towel
- ☑ Heavy book
- ☑ Acrylic paint in various colors
- ☑ PVA glue
- ☑ 4 or 5 small, strong magnets
- ☑ Strong glue

1 Pour the milk into a saucepan, then stir in the vinegar.

2 Place the saucepan on the stove and heat on a high temperature, without stirring, until the milk and vinegar start separating. This will take around a minute.

3 Stir the mixture so that the white parts separate from the clear parts and start to clump up.

4 When it has cooled down completely, squeeze out any moisture from the clump on the side of the pan, and place onto a piece of greaseproof paper. This is called casein.

5 Don't mold the mixture too much or it will dry out. Roll it out on the greaseproof paper until it is nice and thin, then use the cookie cutters to cut out shapes.

6 Place the shapes between two pieces of kitchen towel, then put a heavy book on top. Leave for a couple of days to dry out. The weight of the book will stop the plastic from curling up.

7 Use acrylic paint on the shapes in colors and patterns of your choice. Add a coat of PVA glue if you want a bit of extra shine.

8 Glue strong magnets onto the back.

SCIENCE MADE SIMPLE

CASEIN is a **PROTEIN** found in milk. When the milk and vinegar are heated up, a **CHEMICAL REACTION** occurs. The **ACID** in the vinegar makes contact with the proteins in the milk. The small casein molecules join together to make longer chains called **POLYMERS**. These long chains don't mix with the vinegar, so instead they form clumps. These clumps of protein can then be molded together to make a type of **BIOPLASTIC**.

Plastic is usually made from **PETROLEUM**, but this is a huge problem for our planet, with mountains of plastic waste building up in our oceans and in landfill. Bioplastic, made from plant-based materials like corn starch or sugar cane, is becoming more popular as a greener option. However, some people think that using fewer throwaway items is a better solution.

Ice Rescue

We all know that on a hot summer day an ice cube in your drink melts very fast due to the heat. But it's not just heat that can melt ice. This experiment is a great way to learn what speeds up the melting process, while rescuing toys at the same time!

YOU WILL NEED

- ☑ Water for freezing
- ☑ Small plastic containers, silicon molds or ice-cube tray
- ☑ Small plastic toys (small enough to fit in containers)
- ☑ Salt
- ☑ Sugar
- ☑ Warm water for melting
- ☑ Baking soda (bicarbonate of soda)
- ☑ Teaspoon

Tip

If you've used an ice-cube tray, you can use a different substance for each block of ice and use a timer to see which substance takes the least amount of time to melt the ice.

1 Begin by filling up your container or mold with water. Pop your chosen toys into the water.

2 Place the mold in the freezer overnight and then remove the ice the next day.

3 Put the salt, sugar, warm water, and baking soda into separate containers. Start to sprinkle each substance over the ice, using a teaspoon, and watch what happens to the ice for each one.

4 Keep adding different substances to melt the ice and rescue the toys.

Tip

As a control, keep one ice block untreated to see how long it would take to melt at room temperature. You could even make predictions beforehand to see which substances will speed up the melting process.

SCIENCE MADE SIMPLE

Ice begins to melt and turn from a **SOLID** to a **LIQUID** as soon as you take it out of the freezer. The **HEAT ENERGY** in the room starts breaking it down and turning it back to water. You can speed this up by using a few simple kitchen cupboard ingredients. Hot water is a higher temperature than the ice so the heat energy is transferred to the ice and melts it.

Salt makes the **MELTING POINT** of water lower. This means the temperature that a liquid freezes at can be changed. Pure water freezes at 32°F (0°C). By using salt, that melting point can be lowered, which prevents the water from freezing or re-freezing. Baking soda and sugar work in a similar way.

Ice (solid) → Melting point → Water (liquid)

Melting point is lowered by adding salt

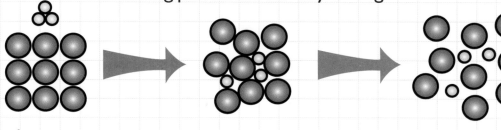

Saltwater ice → Salty slush → Saltwater

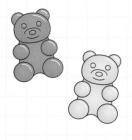

Growing Gummy Bears

This is a quick and simple experiment that will teach you about the process of osmosis. We have used gummy bears but you can have a go with any type of gelatin-based candy to get the same results.

YOU WILL NEED

- ☑ 4 small glass containers (small drinking glasses or jars)
- ☑ Boiling water
- ☑ 2 tbsp salt
- ☑ 2 tbsp sugar
- ☑ ½ cup white vinegar
- ☑ Paper and sticky tape for labels
- ☑ 4 gummy bears (or any gelatin-based candy)

Safety note

Don't eat the gummy bears after you have finished. Harmful bacteria may have grown inside them during the experiment. Keep a few spare in the packet for eating while you wait for the results.

1 Ask an adult to help pour boiling water into one of the glass containers. Add 1 tbsp of sugar and stir well until dissolved, then repeat to add 2 tbsp in total.

2 Repeat step 1 using salt instead of sugar. Label the two containers and put them both in the fridge for an hour to cool completely.

3 Take the remaining two containers and fill one with cold water and the other with vinegar, then add labels to each of the containers so that you can easily identify each one.

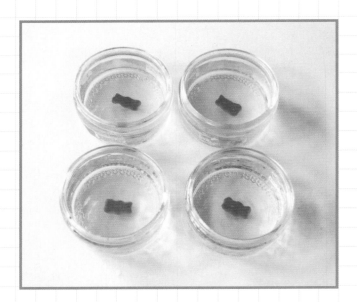

4 Add a gummy bear to each container. It helps to use the same color for each one to easily compare the results. Place the containers on a shelf. After a few hours you can check them. Are there any changes yet? Leave them for 24 hours to see what happens.

5 The next day, check on your experiment. Use a spoon to remove them from the liquids and have a look to see what has happened. Compare your gummies to an unsoaked bear from the packet. In our experiment the water-soaked bear more than doubled in size overnight, the saltwater bear shrank, and the vinegar bear dissolved.

SCIENCE MADE SIMPLE

Osmosis is the **MOVEMENT** of water from an area of high concentration to one of low concentration through a **SEMI-PERMEABLE MEMBRANE** (a type of barrier). It tries to make the water concentrations the same on both sides.

Gummy bears are made of gelatin and a type of sugar called **SUCROSE**. The gelatin stops the sweets from dissolving in water and helps them hold their structure. (See page 61 for more about gelatin.) The surface of the gelatin behaves like a semi-permeable membrane. It acts like a net with small holes that allows smaller particles, like water, to pass through into the bear, but the holes are too small to let the sucrose out of the bear. In the experiment, the gummy bear put in plain tap water has a lower concentration of water than the surrounding water. The water **MOLECULES** pass easily through the gelatin and the bear absorbs the water, growing bigger like a sponge. With more water inside, it becomes softer and squishier.

When the gummy bear is put into a concentrated sugar or salt solution the differences between the two concentrations is much smaller and so the bear does not grow as much. You may even see that the bear shrinks a little in the salt solution. You probably noticed that your poor vinegar bear lost its shape altogether. This is because the gelatin started to be dissolved by the **ACIDS** in the vinegar.

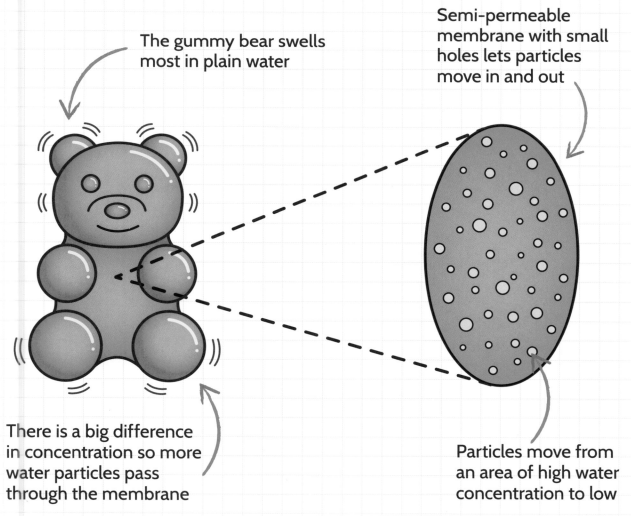

The gummy bear swells most in plain water

Semi-permeable membrane with small holes lets particles move in and out

There is a big difference in concentration so more water particles pass through the membrane

Particles move from an area of high water concentration to low

Salad Spinner Art

Make some colorful artwork and learn all about forces at the same time. Using something you wash your salad greens in is a fun way to have a science lesson!

YOU WILL NEED

- ☑ Salad spinner
- ☑ Acrylic paint in a few different colors
- ☑ Card stock in a color of your choice
- ☑ Scissors
- ☑ Adhesive putty

Tip

For this project, it's best to use an old salad spinner that you can keep just for arts and crafts. Don't try and wash your lettuce leaves in it after this activity!

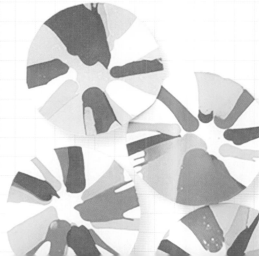

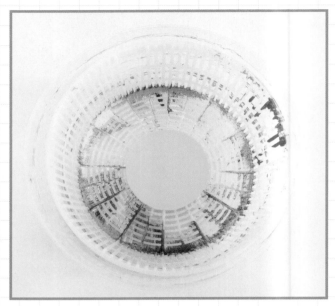

1 Start by cutting out a shape from the card stock. We cut circles. The shape needs to be small enough to fit, laid flat, into the base of the salad spinner.

2 Use a piece of adhesive putty to stick the card onto the base of the spinner, in the center.

3 Add a few drops of different-colored paint onto the card. The paint should be quite runny so it will move when spun. If necessary, you could thin your paint to the right consistency with water before starting.

4 Put the lid on the spinner and give it a good spin.

5 If you like you can add more dollops of paint or a sprinkle of glitter and spin again to build up the effect.

Tip

Acrylic paint works best for this project as it is the right consistency. Make sure you cover your work surfaces and clothing as it can stain.

SCIENCE MADE SIMPLE

When the salad spinner is being spun, there is a **FORCE** acting toward the middle of the spinner. This is called **CENTRIPETAL FORCE**. This is also the force on a ball attached to a string being swung around in a circle and the force acting on the Earth while it is orbiting around the Sun.

The salad spinner also has **VELOCITY** that acts sideways, like it's trying to escape from the circle it's moving in. The velocity pulls the paint outward in straight lines as the spinner spins.

You can feel the effect of centripetal force and velocity on merry-go rounds and roundabouts. If you go very fast, it feels as if you are being pulled outward, just like the paint in the salad spinner.

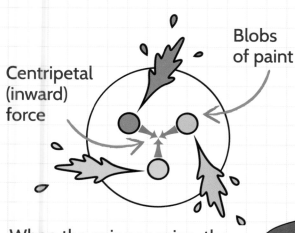

Centripetal (inward) force

Blobs of paint

When the spinner spins, the paint gets flung outward

Centripetal force and velocity make it feel like you are being pulled outward

Egg in a Bottle

How can you get an egg inside a glass bottle without pushing it in? This experiment is well worth the time it takes to hard-boil an egg and the amazing results are all thanks to air pressure.

YOU WILL NEED

- ☑ Hard-boiled egg with the shell removed
- ☑ Glass bottle or jar with a rim slightly smaller than an egg
- ☑ Strip of newspaper or paper (or matches)
- ☑ Lighter (long-handled ones work well)
- ☑ Fork

Safety note

Ask an adult to help with using the lighter or matches.

1 Place the peeled, hard-boiled egg next to the jar and you will notice that it won't fit in the neck.

2 Ask an adult to light the end of the newspaper strip and quickly place it inside the jar, as far as it will go. While the flame is still burning, quickly place the egg on top of the jar.

3 The egg should start to wiggle and vibrate, and will slowly move and be sucked into the jar all by itself!

4 Air pressure got the egg into the bottle and it can also get it out again! Use a fork to remove the paper in the bottle so it doesn't get in the way for the next step.

5 Hold the bottle upside down and move the egg around until the smaller end is in the neck of the bottle. Cover the bottle's opening with your mouth and blow as much air as you can into it. Quickly remove from your mouth. The egg should pop out of the bottle.

SCIENCE MADE SIMPLE

So how did the egg move into the bottle without anyone touching it? It's all because of **AIR PRESSURE**. Before the lit piece of newspaper is put inside the bottle, the air pressure inside and outside it is the same. When the lit piece of newspaper was put into the bottle and the egg put on top, the egg acted as a seal so the air inside the bottle heats up and **EXPANDS**. The egg wiggles as some of the expanding air escapes the bottle. The flame goes out because it has run out of oxygen and the air begins to cool and **CONTRACT** inside the bottle, making the air pressure inside less than the air pressure outside the bottle. Air likes to move from high to low pressure so the air outside pushes the egg into the bottle as it moves from high to low pressure.

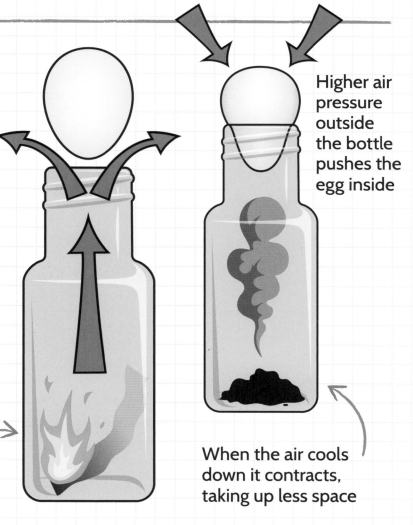

Higher air pressure outside the bottle pushes the egg inside

Air expands in the bottle as it warms up and escapes out the top

When the air cools down it contracts, taking up less space

Microwave Teacup Cakes

Have you ever cooked a cake in just one minute? These yummy and super-speedy treats are a perfect rainy-day activity, and you can learn all about how microwaves work at the same time.

Tip

You could make many variations of this cake. Add 1 tbsp of cocoa and reduce the flour to 2¼oz (60g) for a delicious chocolate cake, or swap the vanilla extract for lemon or almond.

YOU WILL NEED

(makes two chocolate-chip teacup cakes)

- ☑ 1¼oz (35g) butter
- ☑ 1¾oz (50g) superfine (caster) sugar
- ☑ 1 egg
- ☑ ½ tsp vanilla extract
- ☑ 2 tbsp milk
- ☑ 2½oz (70g) all-purpose (plain) flour
- ☑ ¼ tsp baking powder
- ☑ 1¼oz (35g) chocolate chips
- ☑ Confectioners' (icing) sugar, for sprinkling
- ☑ Jug
- ☑ Microwave-safe teacups or mugs
- ☑ Microwave oven
- ☑ Spoon
- ☑ Whisk

1 Place the butter in a jug and heat in the microwave for 30 seconds to melt.

2 Add the sugar and the egg, then whisk to combine. Mix in the vanilla extract and milk, then fold in the flour and baking powder.

3 Mix in the chocolate chips. At this point, you can cover the mixture and leave it in the fridge for up to two days.

4 Divide the mixture between two teacups so that they are two-thirds full.

5 Place the teacups in the microwave individually and heat on full power for one minute. If the cake still looks wet, cook for another 20 seconds or so.

6 Dust with confectioners' sugar and serve warm.

SCIENCE MADE SIMPLE

MICROWAVES are invisible waves of **ENERGY**, just like radio waves. They are called "micro" because they have shorter **WAVELENGTHS** and have a higher frequency. Microwave ovens are named after the wavelength they use to operate. As well as heating food, microwaves have many uses, including radar and satellite communication.

Microwave ovens contain a small **TRANSMITTER** that sends waves of energy into the food. The waves hit the **MOLECULES** of water and make them move around rapidly and warm up. This is how microwave ovens cook food so fast.

The discovery that microwaves can heat food was actually a complete accident! In 1946 an American engineer called Percy Spencer was working on some radar equipment when he noticed that the microwaves melted a snack bar he had in his pocket. The next day he returned with corn kernels and discovered he could make popcorn with the machine! Percy had accidentally discovered a new, fast way to cook food and the microwave oven was born.

Water molecules in the food move around causing it to heat up

Microwaves bounce around inside the oven

Wave transmitter

Candy Rainbow

This quick and easy experiment is like a mesmerizing work of art. Grab a pack of candy and prepare to be dazzled by the swirling colors and patterns you can create. Diffusion is the science word for this amazing display.

YOU WILL NEED

- ☑ Any type of brightly colored, hard-coated candy
- ☑ Jug
- ☑ Warm water
- ☑ Plate

Tip

You don't have to stick to just one type of candy—why not try a mixture to see how the results differ?

1 Arrange the candy around the edge of a plate. You could alternate the colors or put them in blocks.

2 Pour a little warm water in so that the bottom of the plate is covered.

3 Stand back and watch as the colors from the hard coating bleed out into the center of the plate to create a beautiful rainbow pattern.

SCIENCE MADE SIMPLE

The hard coating on this candy is made up of food coloring and sugar, both of which are great at **DISSOLVING** in water. Once the candy gets wet, you'll start to see the color bleed into the water, then spread out by a process called **DIFFUSION**.

This is where one **SUBSTANCE** spreads or moves freely through another substance. It happens when an area of **HIGHLY CONCENTRATED MOLECULES** move to an area of **LOWER CONCENTRATION**.

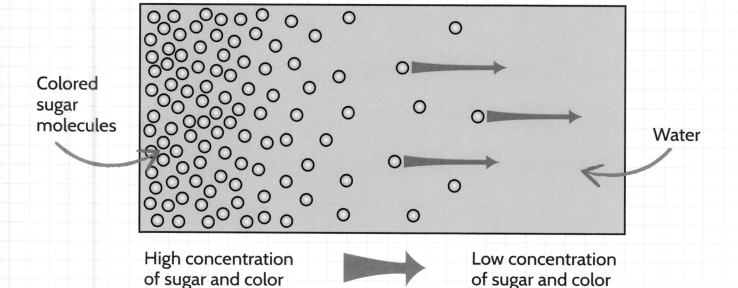

Colored sugar molecules

Water

High concentration of sugar and color

Low concentration of sugar and color

Color-Spectrum Jello

This wobbly wonder is really simple to make but takes a while to create each layer, with setting time in the fridge needed for each one. The finished effect is worth the effort, and you can discover the weird properties of gelatin while you wait.

YOU WILL NEED

- ☑ 1½oz (40g) each of purple, blue, green, yellow, and red jello (jelly) powder
- ☑ 5 tsp gelatin powder
- ☑ Boiling water and cold water
- ☑ Jug
- ☑ Spoon
- ☑ Square glass dish about 10 x 10in (25 x 25cm)
- ☑ Knife
- ☑ Chopping board

Tip

Check the ratio of powder to water for the brand of jello powder you use as it may differ slightly to the one stated in these instructions. Go with the instructions on your packet.

1 Mix 1½oz (40g) of purple jello powder and 1 tsp gelatin powder in a jug with half a cup of boiling water. The gelatin makes the mixture a little bit firmer than regular jello. Stir until dissolved then add half a cup of cold water.

2 Pour the mixture into the dish and place it in the fridge to set for about an hour, making sure the dish is completely flat.

3 Repeat this for the blue, green, yellow, and lastly the red jello mixture. Layer the new color over the previous one each time and then set in the fridge.

4 Once completely set, place the dish in warm water for a minute or two to loosen the jello, then go around the edge with a knife.

5 Place a chopping board on top of the dish and quickly turn it upside down. It should plop right out. If not, give it a few taps to loosen it, or sit it back in the warm water for another minute.

6 Trim off the edges of the jello to tidy them up. Now you will start to see the beautiful layers of color.

7 Chop the jello into cubes. Serve and enjoy! You can keep it in the fridge for up to a week.

SCIENCE MADE SIMPLE

What makes jello wobble? The main ingredient of jello is **GELATIN**, which is a type of **PROTEIN** made from animal bones. When gelatin is heated, the protein fibers break up, making it more watery. You can see that the jello powder and hot water are a **LIQUID**. When you cool it down in the fridge, the protein fibers reattach to each other, but this time they trap water between them. The jello sets, but the high water content makes it very wobbly.

Protein fibers break apart when heated

The fibers reattach with water trapped between them to make the jello wobble

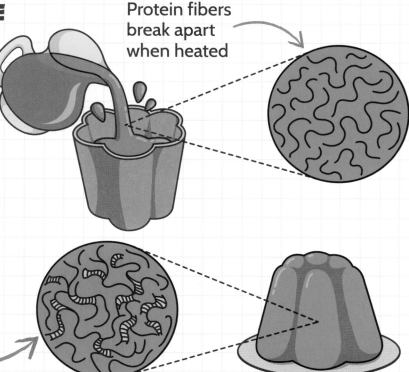

Bunny Bread Buns

These bunny buns are a very tasty way to learn all about how yeast works and are great fun to make. Cook up a batch and then impress your friends with the science know-how you have discovered.

YOU WILL NEED

- ☑ 17oz (500g) strong white bread flour
- ☑ 2¼oz (60g) butter at room temperature
- ☑ 1½oz (40g) superfine (caster) sugar
- ☑ 1 tsp salt
- ☑ ¼oz (7g) (usually 1 sachet) fast-action dried yeast
- ☑ 2 eggs
- ☑ 7 fl oz (200ml) milk
- ☑ Plastic wrap
- ☑ Scissors
- ☑ Black food coloring pen

Tip

You can make other animal-shaped buns: Snip all the way down the back of the bread to make a hedgehog, roll your dough into a spiral to make a snail, or add two small balls of dough for ears to make a bear.

1 Sift the flour into a bowl and use your fingers to mix in the butter.

2 Add the sugar, salt, and yeast and stir to combine. The yeast is the most important ingredient in this recipe. It will make your bread rise and turn your bunnies into fluffy, tasty buns rather than inedible rocks!

3 Beat the eggs a little to combine. Heat the milk in a microwave for 30 seconds to warm. Pour the eggs and milk into the flour and mix together to form a dough.

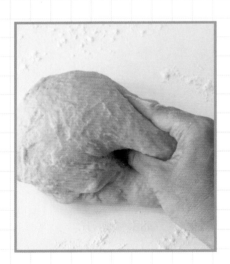

4 Turn the dough out onto a clean, floured work surface and use your hands to knead the dough for 10 minutes, until it goes smooth and stretchy. This will make your dough soft and strong.

5 Place back in the bowl, cover with plastic wrap and leave in a warm place to rise for an hour.

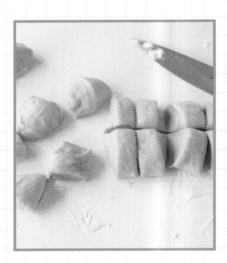

6 Knock the air out of the dough and roll it into a fat sausage. Chop it in half, then in half again until you get 12 roughly equal-sized pieces.

7 Roll each of the pieces into an egg shape. Place onto a lined baking sheet, then cover lightly with plastic wrap and leave for another hour in a warm place.

8 Once risen, preheat the oven to 450°F (230°C). Using scissors, snip two ear shapes into the dough. Round the ends with your fingers.

9 Bake for 12–15 minutes or until golden brown. Once cooled, use a black food coloring pen to mark a little nose and some eyes on the bunnies.

SCIENCE MADE SIMPLE

Most bread recipes use **YEAST**. It is what causes the bread buns to (hopefully) rise up so beautifully. Yeast is a **MICROORGANISM**, a very small life form. This means it is actually alive. When you combine yeast with warmth, water, and flour it thrives. As it does so, it converts the sugar and the starch from the flour into alcohol and makes **CARBON DIOXIDE (CO_2)**. The CO_2 forms air bubbles in the dough and makes it rise. When the dough is placed in a hot oven the yeast organisms are destroyed.

The yeast creates bubbles of CO_2 in the dough, causing the bread to rise

Electric oobleck

Have you heard of oobleck? It is a wonderfully gooey mix of cornstarch and water that is half solid and half liquid. The name was invented by Dr Seuss, and it refers to a non-Newtonian fluid that acts like both a solid and a liquid. Have fun experimenting with static electricity and this lovely substance.

YOU WILL NEED

- ☑ 1 balloon
- ☑ ½ cup cornstarch (cornflour)
- ☑ 1–1½ fl oz (30–40ml) water
- ☑ Gel food coloring
- ☑ Cocktail stick
- ☑ Spoon

Tip

Put your oobleck into a zip-seal bag. Flatten out the bag then squish it around with your fingers, or use a lollipop stick to write messages and draw pictures. Still lots of fun, but less messy!

1 Pour the cornstarch into a bowl and mix in the water. The mixture should have a consistency that is a little difficult to get a spoon through, but also falls back to a smooth surface.

2 Try rolling the mixture between your fingers. Leave it there for a minute and see what happens. When you move it around quickly it acts like a solid, but when it is left to rest, it dribbles and behaves like a liquid.

3 Add a few drops of food coloring using a cocktail stick. Pick colors that will blend well together, like yellows and reds, so that you don't end up with a murky brown. Notice that the colors don't bleed into the mixture like they would with an ordinary liquid. Play around with mixing the oobleck and see how the colors swirl and marble to make new ones.

4 Blow up a balloon and rub it against your head until you feel your hair start to "stick" to it. Take a spoonful of oobleck and, holding the balloon near the spoon, let the mixture drizzle down. You should see that it bends toward the static balloon as it drips. This is better with small thin drizzles, so if your mixture is too thick add a little more water.

MORE FUN WITH STATIC ELECTRICITY

What else has a static pull? Experiment by tearing up some paper into tiny pieces. Rub the balloon in your hair then place it close to the paper. What happens? You should see that the static in the balloon picks up some of the paper.

You could also try pouring a little salt and pepper onto a plate. Mix it around a little then hold the balloon over it. The balloon should pick the pepper up! Or why not try holding it next to a trickling tap to see if you can make the water bend like the oobleck did?

SCIENCE MADE SIMPLE

Oobleck is a **NON-NEWTONIAN FLUID**. That means that, unlike normal fluids, it changes its consistency based on the pressure you put on it. When you stir it, or add pressure, it thickens. With less pressure, it behaves more like a **LIQUID**. This is because the cornstarch particles are a solid that are held in **SUSPENSION** in the water. When you apply pressure, they stick together and trap the water **MOLECULES**.

But why does it bend toward the balloon? This is because of **STATIC ELECTRICITY**. This is an electric charge that has built up on an object. The balloon gets charged from being rubbed on your hair: the **ELECTRONS** (or negatively charged particles) move from your hair to the balloon. Water molecules have a positive side and negative side.

When the negative balloon is near the water, the positive side of the water molecules in the oobleck are attracted to it. The water molecules line up so that all the positive sides are near the balloon. This pulls the oobleck toward it.

In the same way, the little bits of paper are attracted to the charged balloon and jump up to attach to it. For the salt and pepper, the balloon only picks up the pepper because the pepper particles are lighter than the salt.

Negatively charged particles from rubbing the balloon on your hair

Water molecules line up so their positive side is nearest to the balloon

Floating Eggs

How can you make an egg float in the middle of a glass of water? With a little bit of science and a little bit of salt!

YOU WILL NEED

- ☑ 3 eggs (uncooked)
- ☑ Water
- ☑ 3 large empty glasses/jars all the same size
- ☑ About 15 tbsp table salt
- ☑ Spoon
- ☑ Jug

1 Fill two large glasses three quarters with water and pour a generous amount of salt (around 10 tbsp) into one of the glasses. Leave the other glass as plain water.

2 Stir the salt into the water with a spoon to let it dissolve.

3 Drop an uncooked egg into each glass. What do you think will happen? Will the saltwater or plain water make the egg float or sink?

4 Let the eggs settle. You'll probably notice the egg in saltwater floats and the egg in plain water sinks. If it doesn't, add a little more salt.

5 Half fill the remaining glass with water and stir in about 5 tbsp of salt. Stir to dissolve.

6 Drop an uncooked egg into the glass as before. You should see that it floats in the water.

7 Slowly top up the glass with tap water to the same level as the other glasses, using a jug. Let it trickle down one side of the glass to slowly pour it in. Now you should notice that the egg in half salt/half plain water floats in the middle of the glass.

SCIENCE MADE SIMPLE

Some objects float in water and some sink. How well something floats is called **BUOYANCY**. If they sink or float depends on **DENSITY**. This is the **MASS** of something in the space it occupies.

An egg tends to float in saltwater, sink in plain water and be somewhere in the middle with a mix of both. This is because the density of the uncooked egg is higher than tap water, so the egg will sink to the bottom of the glass. When you add salt to the water you increase the density of it. The density of the water is higher than the egg's so the egg floats at the top of the water.

The egg that floated in the middle of the glass has a mix of salt and plain water. The egg floats in the middle of the glass because the egg is more dense than the plain water at the top but less dense than the saltwater at the bottom.

Plain water is less dense than saltwater, with more spaced out particles

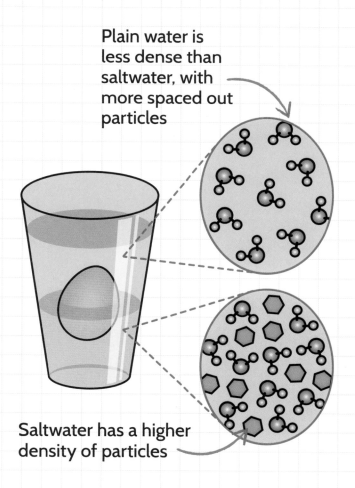

Saltwater has a higher density of particles

Popping Candy Balloons

Is it possible to blow up a balloon without using any puff? This cool trick will dazzle your friends and you can explain to them how the science works.

YOU WILL NEED

- ☑ 2 packets of popping candy
- ☑ Small bottle of any carbonated (fizzy) drink
- ☑ Small funnel
- ☑ Balloon

1 Open the packet of popping candy and use a small funnel to pour the candy into the balloon.

2 Twist the neck of the balloon so the popping candy doesn't fall out. Stretch the end of the balloon over the neck of the bottle. Make sure it is on securely with no gaps and is positioned evenly over the bottle.

3 Untwist the balloon so the popping candy falls into the drink. Watch the balloon self-inflate as the reaction happens!

SCIENCE MADE SIMPLE

Popping candy contains pressurized **CARBON DIOXIDE (CO_2)**. The popping sound you hear when you eat it is this **GAS** escaping.

The soda drink is a carbonated liquid, which also contains a lot of pressurized carbon dioxide gas. When the popping candy is dropped into the drink, the gas from the soda collects on the surface of the popping candy. Some of the gas escapes from the water and corn syrup in the drink and moves upward through the liquid and then into the balloon to inflate it.

Water magic

This experiment may look like a magic trick at first, but once you learn about the density and movement of water molecules you will see how amazing simple science can be.

YOU WILL NEED

- ☑ Warm and cold water
- ☑ 2 empty drinking glasses (the same size)
- ☑ Red and blue food coloring
- ☑ Thick piece of card stock (a little bigger than the rim of the glass)

Safety note

Do not use scalding water for this experiment as the glass will get too hot to touch and it may spill and cause burns. Warm water will work just as well.

Tip

You can use any thick card stock for this experiment. We used a silver one for a bit more resistance to the water. Thin card will get a bit soggy and probably break.

1 Make sure you are on a surface where it doesn't matter if there are any spills. Fill two matching glasses, one with warm water and one with cold water.

2 Add red food coloring to the warm water and blue food coloring to the cold water. Mix in, then top up the glasses so that the water goes right to the brim.

3 Take the piece of card and place it over the top of the cold-water glass. Flip it upside down and carefully remove your hand. The card should stay in place.

4 Place the upside-down cold-water glass on top of the warm water glass. Place it so that the rims line up exactly.

5 Very carefully, slide the card out, keeping the rims lined up as you go. You should see that the water mixes together to create purple.

6 Tip out this water and start again, repeating steps 1 to 4, but this time put the card onto the warm water glass, tip this upside down and place it on top of the cold water. This time red is on top and blue is at the bottom.

7 Carefully pull out the card again to see what happens this time. You should see that the red and blue colors aren't really mixing at all and remain mostly separate in their glasses.

SCIENCE MADE SIMPLE

In the first part of this experiment, you put the cold water on top of the warm. The two **LIQUIDS** mixed together when the card was removed. The warm water rose from the bottom glass to the top and the cold water sank. This is because warm water is less dense than cold water. **DENSITY** is the mass of something in the space it occupies.

When water is heated up, the **MOLECULES** speed up and move around quickly. They hit each other and move farther apart than when they are cold. The molecules are less tightly packed together, which makes the warm water less dense than cold water.

When you repeat the experiment with the warm water on top, the less dense of the two liquids is already at the top, so they do not mix as much.

Warm water molecules move around faster, bouncing off each other, and are less dense

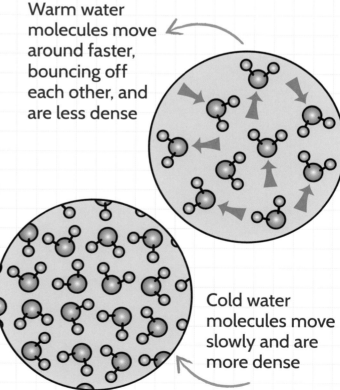

Cold water molecules move slowly and are more dense

Lemon Battery

When you've run out of battery power, instead of heading to the shops, head to the kitchen instead! This simple experiment will introduce the wonders of electricity and you can easily get all the materials needed online.

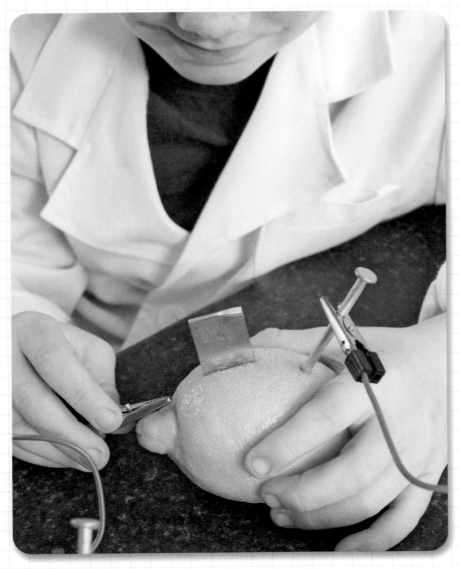

YOU WILL NEED

- ☑ 4 lemons
- ☑ 4 pieces of copper (coin, wire or small sheet)
- ☑ Galvanized nails (zinc coated)
- ☑ 5 wired and double-ended alligator (crocodile) clips with wires
- ☑ Small LED light

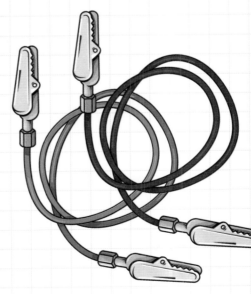

1 Start by rolling the lemons on a work surface to break up the pulp inside them.

2 Push a piece of copper into one side of each lemon so it breaks the skin and is embedded into the lemon. Here we are using copper sheet but you could use a coin or copper wire. On the opposite side, push in a galvanized nail.

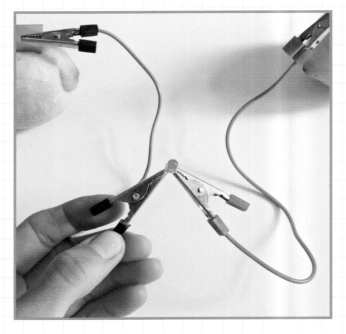

3 Clip one end of a double-ended alligator clip onto the copper in one lemon and the other end onto the nail in another lemon. Work your way around the lemons to create a circuit.

4 Attach the last alligator clip to an LED bulb to complete the circuit and light up the bulb. You need a complete circuit to keep the energy going around to light up the bulb.

SCIENCE MADE SIMPLE

To make the bulb light up, an **ELECTRIC CURRENT** has to flow through the circuit (or loop). This happens when **ELECTRONS** move through the wires. To make them move, we need **ENERGY**.

Lemons contain citric **ACID**. When the copper and zinc (from the galvanized nail) are stuck into the lemon, a **CHEMICAL REACTION** happens between the zinc and the acid. This reaction releases energy and makes electrons move through the wires. When the electrons pass through the bulb, the energy is transferred to the bulb, making it light up.

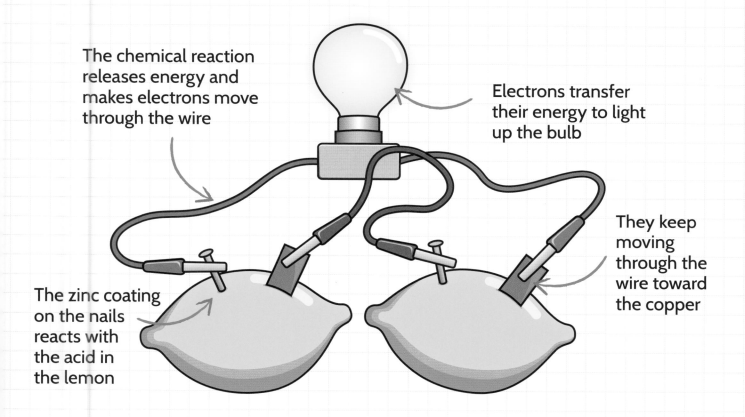

The chemical reaction releases energy and makes electrons move through the wire

Electrons transfer their energy to light up the bulb

They keep moving through the wire toward the copper

The zinc coating on the nails reacts with the acid in the lemon

Tip

If you don't have lemon in the fruit bowl then you can try out other fruits and vegetables. You want ones that are not squishy in the middle. Potatoes work well! Why not experiment with different things to see which gives the best power? Would this also work if you only had one or two lemons or can you use more lemons and add in another LED bulb into the circuit?

Fizzing Candy Dip

This fizzy powdered candy is so easy to make, all you need to do is mix the ingredients together. Dip in some delicious lemon lollipops and feel the tangy fizz. A very tasty chemistry lesson about how an acid and base react together and the science behind molten sugar.

YOU WILL NEED

For the lollipops

- ☑ 5¼oz (150g) superfine (caster) sugar
- ☑ 1 tbsp liquid glucose
- ☑ Juice of half a lemon
- ☑ A drop of yellow food coloring
- ☑ About 6 wooden skewers or 12 lollipop sticks
- ☑ Heavy-based saucepan
- ☑ Greaseproof paper
- ☑ Large bowl of cold water
- ☑ Sugar thermometer
- ☑ Spoon

For the powdered candy

- ☑ 2 tbsp red and green jello (jelly) powder (or any colors of your choice)
- ☑ 4 tbsp confectioners' (icing) sugar
- ☑ 2 tsp citric acid (find in craft stores, pharmacies, or the baking aisle in larger supermarkets)
- ☑ 2 tsp baking soda (bicarbonate of soda)
- ☑ 2 bowls
- ☑ Sieve

Safety note

Be careful with making the lollipops–the hot sugar solution can severely burn your skin. This part should be done by an adult.

1 Start by cutting the sharp ends of the wooden skewers off. Then cut each one in half to make a lollipop stick.

2 Measure out all the ingredients for the lollipops into a heavy-based saucepan.

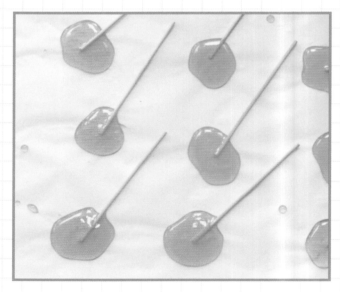

3 Lay out a sheet of greaseproof paper and have a large bowl of cold water ready to cool your mixture. Ask an adult to place the pan on the heat then bring it to the boil. Reduce the heat and simmer until the mixture reaches 300°F (150°C). This will take about five minutes. Use a sugar thermometer to be accurate.

4 Once it reaches the right temperature, ask an adult to immediately dip the pan in the cold water to stop the mixture from burning. Carefully drop blobs of the mixture onto the greaseproof paper. Add the sticks to each blob as you go. Give the sticks a twist to coat them in the mixture and leave to cool.

5 For the powdered candy, measure out the ingredients into two separate bowls. In one bowl, mix the red jello powder with 2 tbsp confectioners' sugar, 1 tsp citric acid, and 1 tsp of baking soda. Repeat in a separate bowl with the green jello powder.

6 Sieve the mixed powders to remove any lumps, then put 1 tbsp of each color into a small bowl and serve with a couple of the lemon lollipops. Think about the fizzing, sugary sensation that hits your tongue. What might be causing it?

SCIENCE MADE SIMPLE

The fizz from powdered candy is caused by a **CHEMICAL REACTION** happening right there on your tongue. The baking soda is a **BASE** and when it is mixed, with the citric **ACID** and the water in your mouth, they react and produce **CARBON DIOXIDE (CO$_2$)**, which is released in the form of lots of tiny bubbles of **GAS**. This makes it tingle and pop on your tongue. (See also the lemon volcanoes on page 28.)

How do the lollipops go from boring dry ingredients to a lovely glass-like hard candy? When sugar is heated up enough it becomes molten. That means it is usually a **SOLID** but becomes a **LIQUID** when it is hot enough. When the liquid sugar cools, it goes hard again and becomes an **AMORPHOUS SOLID**. This means that the molecules have been jumbled up. The result is a clear solid that looks a bit like a liquid, with its glass-like appearance.

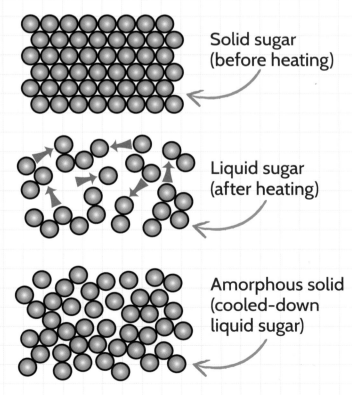

Solid sugar (before heating)

Liquid sugar (after heating)

Amorphous solid (cooled-down liquid sugar)

Salt Paintings

This is a fun activity for a rainy day. The salt absorbs food coloring really well and it's fascinating to watch the colors blend and bleed into each other. Bear in mind that this project will need to be done in two sessions to allow for the glue to dry. You could do it with wet glue, but the salt absorption won't be quite as good.

YOU WILL NEED
- ☑ Pencil
- ☑ Thick card stock
- ☑ Tray
- ☑ PVA glue (in a bottle with a small nozzle)
- ☑ Table salt
- ☑ Red, yellow, and blue food coloring
- ☑ Artists' palette or separate small dishes
- ☑ Paintbrush

1 Sketch out a simple design in pencil onto a piece of card stock.

2 Place the card stock on a tray. Go over the pencil lines using PVA glue. To do this, tip the glue up and let it drizzle through the nozzle along the lines. Fill in the picture with more drizzles.

3 Generously sprinkle salt all over the glue so that the whole design is completely covered. Set this aside to dry for about 24 hours.

4 Once dry, tip off the excess salt and brush it away with your fingers. Discard the salt.

5 Place some food coloring in a palette or separate small dishes. If you are using gel food coloring, mix it with a little water to make a thin consistency. Dip a paintbrush into one of the colors and drop it onto the salt. The color will bleed into the salt and spread.

6 Keep adding other colors randomly onto the salt. Watch as they bleed into the salt and into each other to make new colors.

SCIENCE MADE SIMPLE

The grains of salt absorb and soak up the liquid really easily and spread it around. Salt is **HYGROSCOPIC**, which means it easily absorbs moisture. The colors bleed into the salt and when they meet, they create new colors. That's why using **PRIMARY COLORS** (blue, red, and yellow) is great for this experiment, as they form the basis of other colors. You probably saw some orange, purple, and green forming as the colors joined. These are **SECONDARY COLORS**.

Mixing two primary colors together makes a secondary color ←

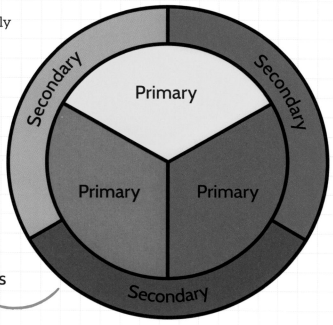

Colorful Cabbage

White cabbage is a great vegetable to learn all about how plants take in water. In this experiment you will learn all about how they do this themselves through a process called transpiration.

YOU WILL NEED

- ☑ 3 empty glass jars
- ☑ Food coloring in different colors
- ☑ White cabbage
- ☑ Spoon
- ☑ Sharp knife

1 Fill up the jars with water and stir food coloring into each jar. Add quite a lot of food coloring to ensure you get a vibrant result.

2 Use a sharp knife to cut the end off the cabbage and remove the leaves.

3 Place the leaves into the different-colored jars with the tips at the top.

4 Leave the jars for a few hours and notice the change in the color of the leaves. Leave them overnight to watch them transform.

Tip

If you don't have cabbage in your fridge, you could try this experiment using stalks of celery or white flowers such as carnations or roses.

SCIENCE MADE SIMPLE

Did you know that plants are very good at taking in water? They absorb water from the soil and transport it all the way up the stem to the leaves. Plants only need a small amount of water to grow, so whatever water is left over evaporates when it reaches the leaves or flowers of the plant. This process is called **TRANSPIRATION**. The water is moved up from the roots through small tubes in the plant called **XYLEM**. These are like tiny straws which the water travels through, up the stem. This process is called **CAPILLARY ACTION**. You can see these processes in action with the cabbages. When you add color to the water you can observe how it moves up the xylem tubes in the cabbage, all the way to the edges.

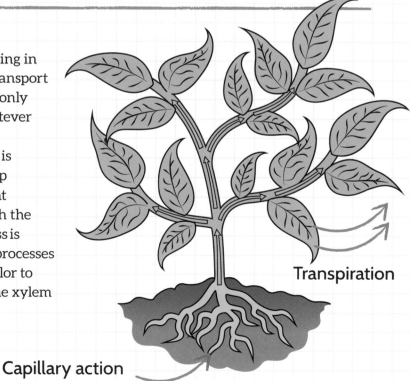

Transpiration

Capillary action

Crush a Can

Can you crush a can without using your hands or feet to squash it? This is a great experiment to learn about how particles behave in liquids and gases and the dramatic "pop" of implosion that happens as a result.

YOU WILL NEED
- ☑ Empty metal soda drinks can
- ☑ Jug
- ☑ Large bowl
- ☑ Ice and cold water
- ☑ Heavy-based skillet (frying pan)
- ☑ Oven gloves
- ☑ Safety goggles
- ☑ Tongs

Safety note
This involves hot temperatures, and we strongly recommend that safety goggles and oven gloves are used. Adults should carry out the crushing part of this experiment.

1 Make sure your soda can is clean and empty. Using a jug, pour in a little water–about 1 tbsp, or so there is about ³/₈in (1cm) in the bottom.

2 Fill a large bowl with ice and cold water. Place this next to the oven so that it is ready.

3 Place the can directly onto the hob on your oven. If you have a gas hob, place the can in a heavy-based skillet. Heat for about five minutes, until you can see steam coming out of it.

4 Wearing safety goggles, pick up the can with the tongs. Quickly plunge the can upside down into the cold water. Prepare for a pop. Your can should now be crushed!

IMPLODING PLASTIC BOTTLE

You can also try the same experiment with an empty plastic soda bottle. Use a funnel to carefully pour a little hot water into the bottle. Seal the top loosely with the cap. The bottle should start to contract (cave inward) as the air gets pushed out the gap at the top of the bottle. When you put it in the icy water it should contract even more as the steam condenses and takes up less room, sucking in the sides of the bottle.

SCIENCE MADE SIMPLE

When the can is heated up, the water inside it boils and turns into steam. The steam pushes the air out of the opening at the top of the can and it fills with steam instead. When the can touches the ice water, a seal is formed over the opening. The steam cools down very quickly and turns back into water, but it takes up far less space than the steam did. No air can get back into the can because the opening is touching the water. As a result, the can **IMPLODES**, meaning it quickly collapses into itself—with a big pop! The air pressure outside the can is now bigger than the pressure inside.

When water turns from a liquid into a gas, the particles become more spaced out as the heat gives them more **ENERGY** to break away from each other, so the steam takes up more space than the water did. Some of the water will also **EVAPORATE** from the opening of the can when it is still on the hob and disappear. When the steam cools down it **CONDENSES** and turns back into a liquid.

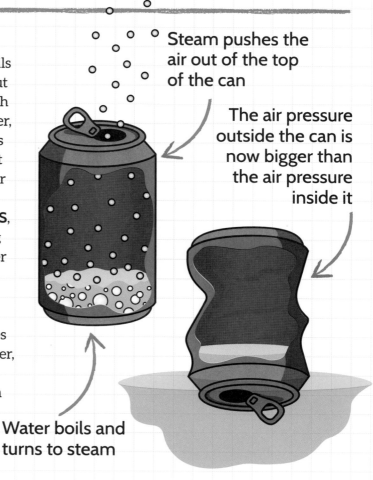

Steam pushes the air out of the top of the can

The air pressure outside the can is now bigger than the air pressure inside it

Water boils and turns to steam

Rainbow Paper

Did you know that you can "catch" a rainbow on black card stock?
It's so easy to do and the results are mesmerizing. The way light travels
in waves creates this colorful effect, which you can also see happening
in nature on an iridescent shell or peacock feather.

YOU WILL NEED
☑ Black card stock
☑ Clear nail varnish
☑ Warm water
☑ Container
☑ Kitchen towel

Tip
Make sure you get both sides of the card wet as the nail varnish will stick to the card better.

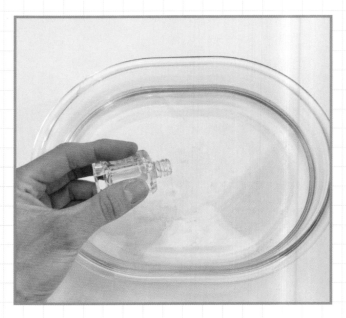

1 Cut out your design from black card stock. We cut out rainbow shapes but you could cut any shape you like.

2 Fill up a container with warm water. The container needs to be big enough to fit the shape. Put a few drops of clear nail varnish into the water. It should sit on the surface of the water.

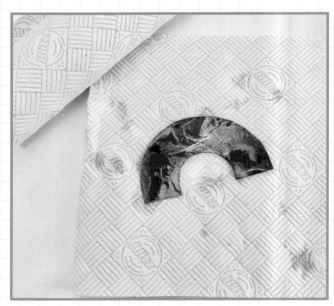

3 Gently place the shape on top of the water pressing down lightly so it gets wet. Pick the shape out of the water and you'll notice it has caught the nail varnish and made a rainbow on the surface.

4 Lay the shape onto a piece of kitchen towel, face up, and leave to dry. Try not to handle it too much.

SCIENCE MADE SIMPLE

When you drop clear nail varnish into water it spreads out and creates a super-thin film on the surface of the water. Nail polish is **HYDROPHOBIC** (repels water) and lighter than water, so the two substances stay separate. It is moved onto the surface of the black card stock but some areas of the film are thicker and some are thinner.

Light travels in **WAVES** and is made up of many **WAVELENGTHS**, which we see as different colors. When light reflects off the thin film of the nail varnish, some areas cause light waves to bounce off the back and the front parts of the film in sync (the peaks of the waves line up) and others become distorted and cancel each other out. The light waves that bounce in sync with each other create bright colors on the surface of the film and the distorted ones show as less bright, or no color at all.

This process is called **THIN-FILM INTERFERENCE**. You can see this in everyday life when an oil slick forms over a puddle on the road or when many colors are seen reflected in a soap bubble. In nature, it is the same process that creates the beautiful iridescent colors seen on bird's feathers or a shiny beetle shell.

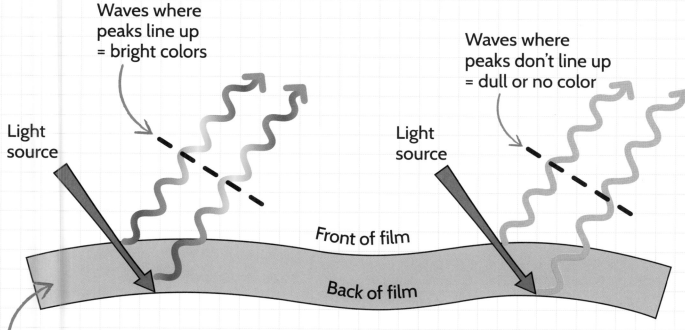

Waves where peaks line up = bright colors

Waves where peaks don't line up = dull or no color

Light source

Light source

Front of film

Back of film

Thin film of clear nail varnish

Red Cabbage Chemistry

Set up your very own chemistry lab in your kitchen using just a red cabbage and a few everyday household products. The juice of a red cabbage is a natural pH indicator. This means that, when added to different substances, it changes color to tell you how acidic they are. Clever stuff!

YOU WILL NEED

- ☑ Red cabbage
- ☑ Chopping board
- ☑ Sharp knife
- ☑ Jug
- ☑ Water
- ☑ Blender
- ☑ Sieve
- ☑ Empty glass jars, one for each substance you want to test
- ☑ A selection of household substances, we used: clear soda drink, hand sanitizer gel, sugar, baking soda (bicarbonate of soda), bleach (use with an adult's supervision), lemon juice, and white vinegar

Safety note

Ask for adult help before using a sharp knife or adding bleach to your cabbage liquid.

1 Start by making the red cabbage solution. Chop up the cabbage into small pieces. We used a couple of handfuls of cabbage.

2 Put the cabbage into a blender, add enough water to cover the cabbage well, and blend together.

3 Push the blended cabbage through a sieve into a jug, to strain the mixture and separate the liquid from the pulp.

4 Pour the cabbage liquid into the jars so they are about one quarter full.

5 Now test the different kitchen substances. Pour or stir a little of each one into the separate jars and watch as the color of the cabbage water changes.

Tip
Try and predict what color you think the cabbage water will turn when you add each substance.

SCIENCE MADE SIMPLE

All solutions are either an **ACID**, a **BASE**, or **NEUTRAL**. An acid is a **CHEMICAL COMPOUND** that has lots of **HYDROGEN IONS**, such as vinegar. A base is the chemical opposite to an acid as it has lots of **HYDROXIDE IONS**, such as baking soda. When an acid and a base are mixed together in the right amounts, they neutralize each other. Water is also known as a neutral substance.

The **PH SCALE** measures how acidic or basic a solution is on a scale of 0–14. A pH indicator, changes color when exposed to acids and bases. Red cabbage juice can be used as a pH indicator because it contains a **PIGMENT** called flavin. Acidic solutions will turn this pigment into a red color because they have a pH of less than 7 on the scale. Neutral solutions result in a purplish color. Base solutions appear in greenish-yellow and have a pH of greater than 7.

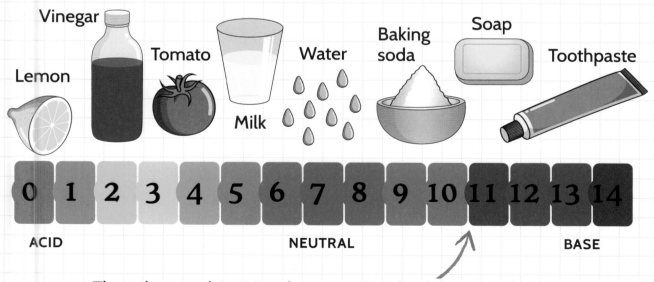

The colors on this pH scale are universal indicators and are different to the ones you will get doing the experiment

Rainbow Window Gems

These window gems are fun to make and look pretty with sunlight shining through them. They also provide a great lesson about diffusion, suction, and how a solid can turn to liquid and back to a solid again.

YOU WILL NEED

- ☑ 1½oz (40g) unflavored gelatin powder
- ☑ 2 cups boiling water
- ☑ Bowl
- ☑ Whisk
- ☑ Cooking oil spray
- ☑ An old baking sheet about 12 x 10in (30 x 25cm)
- ☑ Kitchen towel
- ☑ Food coloring in various colors
- ☑ Cocktail stick
- ☑ Cookie cutters

Tip

After a few days you will notice that the window gems start to shrivel up and harden as the water evaporates out of them. Put them back into water to soak for a while and they can be used again.

1 Add the gelatin powder to a bowl and pour two cups of boiling water on top. Whisk until they are combined.

2 Spray the baking sheet with cooking oil and rub over with kitchen towel to spread it around.

3 Pour the gelatin mixture onto the baking sheet and put aside for a couple of hours to set.

4 Dip a cocktail stick into some food coloring and then poke it into the gelatin in the tray. Use different colors to get a nice pattern. Wipe it down on a cloth each time before going back into the pot. Leave for a couple of hours.

5 You should now see that the food coloring has started to bleed into the gelatin. The colors should start to spread slowly through it.

6 Use cookie cutters to cut shapes from the set gelatin. Place the sticky gem shapes on the window. They will stick all by themselves.

SCIENCE MADE SIMPLE

In this activity, the gelatin changes from a **SOLID** (powder), to a **LIQUID**, to a wobbly solid. This is because the protein fibers in the gelatin are broken up when heated, but they reattach when they cool down and trap water in them. Learn more about the science of gelatin in the color-spectrum jello experiment on page 58.

DIFFUSION is when something spreads out from an area of high concentration to a low concentration. This happens all by itself, without any stirring or other movement needed. The food coloring gradually diffuses through the gelatin. See the candy rainbow experiment on page 56 for more on how diffusion works.

When the sticky gems are first made, they are super soft and stick to the window through **SUCTION**. This is when a slight **VACUUM** is produced. When you push the sticky gems onto the window, you push some of the air out. This vacuum effect is what holds them in place. After a few days they become dehydrated, the water that they contain gradually starts to leave the gems through **EVAPORATION**. This will probably affect the suction and they might fall off.

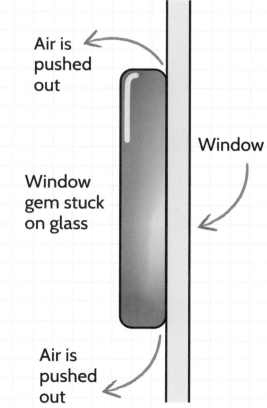

Air is pushed out

Window

Window gem stuck on glass

Air is pushed out

Liquid Density Columns

Not all liquids are the same. Some are thick, gloopy, and pour slowly, like honey. Others are thin and fast-flowing, like water. These colorful layered columns are a great way to learn all about the density of different liquids. This experiment takes a bit of patience to get right as you need to add in each layer very slowly to create the effect.

YOU WILL NEED

For the sugar water column
- ☑ 5 equal-sized empty glass jars or drinking glasses
- ☑ Warm tap water
- ☑ Regular (granulated) sugar
- ☑ Food coloring
- ☑ Spoons
- ☑ Pipette or baster

For the multi-liquid column
- ☑ Large glass
- ☑ 2 pipettes or basters
- ☑ Honey or maple syrup
- ☑ Dishwashing liquid
- ☑ Water (colored with food coloring)
- ☑ Vegetable oil
- ☑ Rubbing alcohol (colored with food coloring)

SUGAR WATER COLUMN

1 Fill up four jars, one-quarter full, with warm tap water and add a few drops of different-colored food coloring to each one. We used blue, green, yellow, and red. Stir to mix the color in.

2 Add 8 tsp of sugar to the blue water. Fill the empty jar one quarter full with blue water.

3 Add 4 tsp of sugar into the green water, mixing well. Fill the pipette with green water and very slowly trickle it into the jar down one of the sides. Doing it very slowly means you don't disturb the layers. Keep adding green water so you have roughly the same amount as the blue.

4 Add 2 tsp of sugar into the yellow liquid and stir well. Clean the pipette and then add the yellow water into the jar slowly, as before.

5 Finally, add 1 tsp of water into the red water. Add the water into the jar in the same way to form the top layer.

Tip

Make sure you stir in each spoonful of sugar well so that it dissolves fully, otherwise the experiment may not work.

MULTI-LIQUID COLUMN

Pour the honey in first, straight down the middle of the glass, so that it doesn't run down the sides. Slowly pour in about the same amount of dishwashing liquid in the same way, it should sit nicely on top. Using a pipette or baster, slowly drop the colored water down the side of the glass on top of the dishwashing liquid. Use a separate pipette to add the vegetable oil on top of the water and then add colored rubbing alcohol to finish.

Tip

If you don't have rubbing alcohol, you can use whole (full fat) milk instead. Add it to the column before the dishwashing liquid.

SCIENCE MADE SIMPLE

DENSITY means how much mass there is in a particular space. When the sugar is added to the water, the sugar **MOLECULES** take up the space between the water molecules, which makes the water more dense. By adding more sugar, you make solutions that have increasing densities.

The densest water (blue) has the most sugar in it and sits at the bottom of the jar. The water with the least sugar (red) is the least dense and sits on top of the other layers.

The same happens in the multi-liquid column. Each one has a different mass of molecules, which gives them different densities. The liquid with the highest density (honey) sits at the bottom. The least dense liquid used, sits at the top.

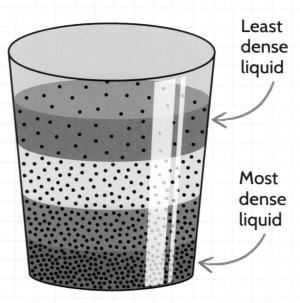

Least dense liquid

Most dense liquid

Density of molecules decreases with each layer

Thermodynamic Ice Pack

This is a quick and easy introduction to thermodynamics and an awesome trick to impress your friends. Magically make an ice pack without adding any ice. Perfect for a hot summer day.

YOU WILL NEED

- ☑ Small zip-seal plastic bag
- ☑ A pin
- ☑ 2 tsp citric acid (find in craft stores, pharmacies, or the baking aisle in larger supermarkets)
- ☑ 3 tsp baking soda (bicarbonate of soda)
- ☑ Jug
- ☑ 2 fl oz (50ml) tap water
- ☑ Thermometer

1 Make a hole in the top of the bag with a pin, wiggling the pin about a bit to make it a little wider. This is to make sure the gases can be released, and the bag doesn't pop.

2 Put 2 tsp citric acid and 3 tsp baking soda into the bag.

3 Pour the tap water into a jug. Feel the temperature with your finger so that you can observe any differences at the end of the experiment. Measure the temperature of the water with a thermometer—our tap water was almost 74°F (23°C).

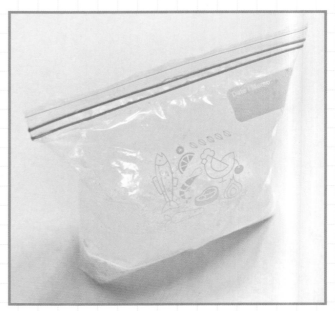

4 Pour the water into the bag. It will fizz and bubble. Seal the bag at the top and it will quickly expand with all the gases that are being released from the chemical reaction that is taking place.

5 Hold the bag in your hand. Does it feel cold? The temperature of the solution should have dramatically dropped, and it should feel very cold now. Open the bag up and test the temperature again. Ours dipped down to 43°F (6°C). That's a huge drop!

Tip

The bag should stay very cold for about 10 minutes. Perfect to cool you down on a hot day.

SCIENCE MADE SIMPLE

THERMODYNAMICS is the science of heat and energy. This experiment is a great example as it can teach us about how **CHEMICAL REACTIONS** cause heat to be taken away (or even added). When the water is added to the mixture, the baking soda and citric **ACID** combine and make a chemical reaction.

This causes **CARBON DIOXIDE (CO_2)** to be released as a gas, which makes the bag puff out. The reaction is also **ENDOTHERMIC**, which means that it absorbs heat from its surroundings. (**EXOTHERMIC** reactions release heat.) In this case, the heat is taken from the water, which is why it becomes colder.

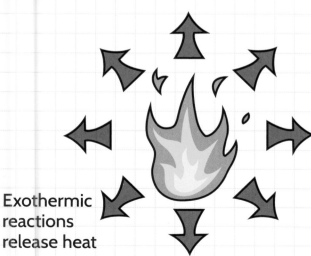

Exothermic reactions release heat

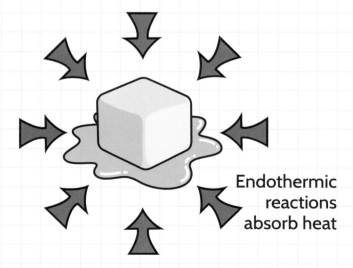

Endothermic reactions absorb heat

Potato Science Tricks

Raid the potato stash in your kitchen and have a go at these simple tricks. Sprouting potatoes are an ideal windowsill experiment to try and you may even end up with a sack-full after a few months! The dehydration activity will get more immediate results for less-patient scientists.

YOU WILL NEED

For spouting potatoes
- ☑ Sweet potato
- ☑ Sharp knife
- ☑ Glass jar, clean and empty
- ☑ Water
- ☑ 4 wooden skewers or cocktail sticks

For dehydrated potatoes
- ☑ White potato
- ☑ Sharp knife
- ☑ Salt
- ☑ Water
- ☑ Two clean and empty containers

SPROUTING SWEET POTATOES

1 Cut the bottom third from the end of the sweet potato using a sharp knife, with the help of an adult.

2 Push four wooden skewers into the potato, about halfway down, spacing them evenly around it. Place it into a jar so the skewers are resting on the rim. It shouldn't touch the bottom.

Tip

When the sprouts have started to grow out the top, you can pinch them off and plant them in the ground, to make new plants. Sweet potatoes love warmth, so make sure the season is right for growing.

3 Fill the jar with water so the cut end of the potato is covered. Check the jar regularly and keep the water topped up so the bottom of the potato stays in water. Leave in a warm sunny spot so it can get lots of sunlight. In a few weeks, roots should start to come out of the sides and sprouts should start to grow out of the top.

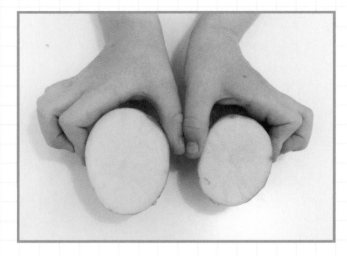

DEHYDRATED POTATOES

1. Cut the potato in half using a sharp knife, with the help of an adult. Fill two containers with about ½in (1.25cm) of water. Add 2 tbsp of salt into one of them (make a note of which one), and stir. Add a potato half to each one and leave for 2–3 hours.

2. What do you notice? You should see that the potato in saltwater looks smaller.

SCIENCE MADE SIMPLE

A sweet potato is a **TUBEROUS ROOT**. This is a type of root that grows big to store nutrients, water, and sugar. This means that the plant can always get what it needs, even during a cold winter or a dry summer. A sweet potato plant also has narrow, fibrous roots that absorb nutrients and water and anchor the plant in the soil. When you put a sweet potato in water, it will sprout shoots. These shoots can be twisted off and grown into new sweet potato plants.

When the dehydrated potatoes are taken out of the water, you'll notice that the one that's been in saltwater is a smaller size to the one in plain tap water. This is because salt has **DEHYDRATED** the potato and drawn the moisture out of it, causing it to shrink. This is done by **OSMOSIS**, a process where water moves from an area of high **CONCENTRATION** to low concentration. Learn more about osmosis on page 43.

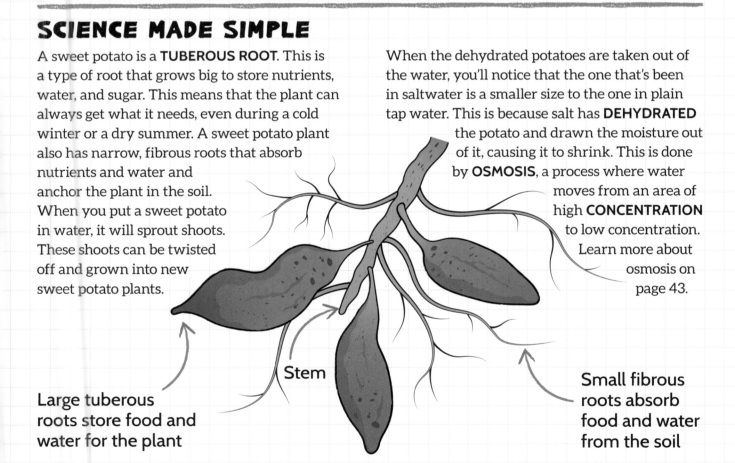

Large tuberous roots store food and water for the plant

Stem

Small fibrous roots absorb food and water from the soil

Glossary

Absorption: Where something takes in or soaks up another substance.

Acid: An acid is a substance that has a pH of less than 7.

Air pressure: The effect of air particles knocking into surfaces or objects.

Alkaline: A solution with a pH that is higher than 7. Alkaline substances are made by dissolving a base.

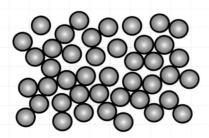

Amorphous solid: Molecules in a solid that have been jumbled up in a disorganized structure, like in a liquid.

Atom: A particle of matter that forms the building block for everything in the Universe. Atoms are made up of electrons, neutrons, and protons.

Base: See Alkaline.

Buoyancy: Tells us how easily something floats. If something is more buoyant, it is more likely to float. The more surface area an object has, the more likely it is to float.

Capillary action: The process by which liquids move through small spaces, like a hollow tube or a spongy material.

Carbon dioxide: A colorless, odorless gas found in our atmosphere. Its chemical formula is CO_2, one carbon atom with two oxygen atoms attached.

Casein: A protein found in milk.

Centripetal force: When objects move in a circle, this force acts toward the center. It stops them flying off, out of the circle.

Chemical energy: Energy stores found in the bonds between atoms.

Chemical reaction: The result of chemicals interacting and converting into other chemicals.

Chemistry: A type of science that looks at chemical elements and compounds and how they work together.

Compound: A compound is two or more different elements chemically bonded together.

Concentration: How much of a substance is mixed with another.

Condense: When a gas cools down and changes into a liquid.

Dehydrate: Losing a lot of water. In your body this means where there is not enough water to work properly.

Density: The mass of an object or substance compared to its volume. If an object is heavy and compact, it has a high density. If an object is light and takes up a lot of space, it has a low density.

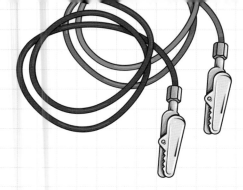

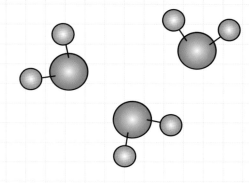

Diffusion: The process where molecules of one substance move from an area where they are in high concentration to an area of low concentration.

Dissolve: To mix completely into a liquid.

Electricity/electric current: The flow of very small particles called electrons and protons.

Electrons: Tiny negatively charged particles that move around inside atoms and electric circuits.

Endothermic reaction: A reaction that takes energy from its surroundings, making it feel colder.

Energy: The ability to cause something around us to change, for example, moving or heating something, or when a chemical reaction happens. A stretched elastic band contains energy because it will ping off when you let go. Energy can be seen and stored in many different forms such as electrical, heat, or chemical.

Exothermic reaction: A reaction that releases heat.

Float: To rest on the surface of a liquid.

Freezing point: The temperature at which a liquid becomes a solid.

Gas: A state of matter where the force between its particles is so small that is has no fixed shape or volume. (See also Liquid, Solid)

Hydrogen: A colorless, odorless, tasteless substance. It is the first element in the Periodic Table.

Hydrophilic: A water-loving substance.

Hygroscopic: A substance that easily absorbs moisture.

Hydroxide: A molecule made up of oxygen and hydrogen.

Implosion: The opposite of an explosion, something that collapses inward.

Liquid: A state of matter with loosely packed particles. The particles can move around and will take the shape of the base of their container. (See also Gas, Solid.)

Mass: The amount of matter that makes up an object.

Microwave: A wave of energy that has a low frequency.

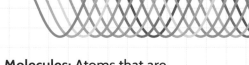

Molecules: Atoms that are connected with bonds.

Neutron: A particle found in an atom that has no electrical charge.

Non-Newtonian fluid: A fluid with viscosity (thickness) that varies depending on the stress or force placed on it.

Osmosis: The flow of water through a semi-permeable membrane from a less-concentrated solution (where there is more water) into a more-concentrated solution (where there is less water).

Oxygen: A colorless, odorless gas. It makes up about one fifth of the air that we breathe in.

Particles: A general name for the incredible small units that everything is made of.

Petroleum: Another name for crude oil. It can be dug up and used to make fuels like petrol and diesel. It can also be used to make plastic.

pH: A scale that measures if a substance is an acid or a base.

Pigment: A substance that adds color to other materials.

Polymer: A long-chain molecule made of lots of smaller molecules.

Primary colors: Colors that cannot be created by mixing together any other colors. In their simplest form they are red, yellow, and blue.

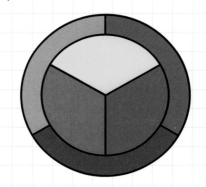

Protein: Long complex molecules that we need for many important processes in our bodies.

Proton: A small positively charged particle found in an atom.

Secondary colors: These can be made by mixing two primary colors together. They are green, orange, and purple. There are also six tertiary colors, which are created by mixing primary and secondary colors together.

Semi-permeable membrane: A thin layer that allows smaller molecules in, but larger ones are blocked.

Sink: When an object falls down to the bottom of a liquid.

Solid: A state of matter that is composed of tightly packed particles, which retain their shapes. (See also Liquid, Gas.)

Solution: A mixture of two or more substances that stay evenly mixed.

Solvent: A substance in which other materials dissolve to form a solution.

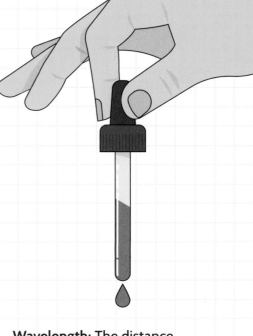

Static electricity: An electrical charge that has built up on an object.

Substance: The material or matter that something is made of.

Suction: The removing of air or water from a space in order to cause something to stick to a surface.

Surface tension: The force that causes a layer of liquid to behave like an elastic sheet.

Thermodynamics: The science of heat and energy.

Thin-film interference: When light waves within layers of a film interfere with each other and alter the light reflected.

Transmitter: A device that sends signals, often using radio waves.

Transpiration: The process by which plants use their roots to absorb water from the soil and carry it up to their leaves.

Tuberous root: A large root that grows big to enable it to store nutrients, water, and sugar.

Vacuum: An area with no air or anything else in it.

Velocity: Tells us how fast an object is moving and its direction.

Wavelength: The distance between two successive crests or troughs of a wave.

Xylem: Small tubes inside a plant that draw up water.

Yeast: A microorganism that helps dough rise.

About the Authors

Laura Minter and Tia Williams are crafters, mothers, and writers. They started *Little Button Diaries*, their award-winning craft blog to show that having children doesn't mean you have to stop doing the things you love. There is always time for crafting (as well as tea and cookies)! They have written many craft books and created craft projects for major retailers Hobbycraft, Paperchase, Brother Sewing, and Duck Tape. Between them, they have five children who they love to make things for (and with!).

Follow them at: www.littlebuttondiaries.com
Twitter: @LButtondiaries
Instagram: @littlebuttondiaries
Tag your photos: #kitchenscience

ACKNOWLEDGMENTS

GMC Publications would like to thank Elinor Rose for her expert knowledge and help. Thanks also to our lovely models: Milo, Charles, Aummie, Diya, Bibi, Kiki, Gracie, Amelie, Harper, Lilah, and Grayson.

First published 2022 by Button Books, an imprint of Guild of Master Craftsman Publications Ltd, Castle Place, 166 High Street, Lewes, East Sussex, BN7 1XU, UK.

ISBN 978 1 78708 122 2

A catalog record for this book is available from the British Library.

Publisher: Jonathan Bailey
Production: Jim Bulley
Senior Project Editor: Virginia Brehaut
Designer: Cathy Challinor

Main photography by Andrew Perris, step-by-step photography by Laura Minter and Tia Williams. All illustrations by Alex Bailey, except on pages: 5 (bottom), 6 (top left and bottom right), 7 (top left), 8 (top right), 13, 14, 18 (top), 52 (top), 56 (top left), 70 (top left), 74, 80 (top left and bottom right), 84, 88, 94, 101 (top right), 102, 105 (bottom), 110, 114, 122 (bottom right, 123 (bottom three), 124 (bottom right), 125 (bottom left and top right) from Shutterstock.com

Color origination by GMC Reprographics.
Printed and bound in China.

Button
BOOKS

For more on Button Books, contact:
GMC Publications Ltd, Castle Place,
166 High Street, Lewes, East Sussex,
BN7 1XU, United Kingdom
Tel: +44 (0)1273 488005
buttonbooks.co.uk
buttonbooks.us